New **Supermarket** Design

New **Supermarket**
Design

Cristian Campos

COLLINS|DESIGN

An Imprint of HarperCollins*Publishers*

First Edition

First published in 2007 by:
Collins Design
An Imprint of HarperCollinsPublishers
10 East 53rd Street
New York, NY 10022
Tel.: (212) 207-7000
Fax: (212) 207-7654
collinsdesign@harpercollins.com
www.harpercollins.com

Distributed throughout the world by:
HarperCollinsPublishers
10 East 53rd Street
New York, NY 10022
Fax: (212) 207-7654

Packaged by:
LOFT Publications
Via Laietana, 32, 4.° Of. 92
08003 Barcelona, Spain
Tel.: +34 932 688 088
Fax: +34 932 687 073
loft@loftpublications.com
www.loftpublications.com

Editor and texts:
Cristian Campos

Editorial Coordination:
Catherine Collin

Translation:
Jay Noden

Art Director:
Mireia Casanovas Soley

Cover:
Claudia Martinez Alonso

Layout:
Yolanda G. Román

Library of Congress Control Number: 2007928596

ISBN-13: 978-0-06-114996-2
ISBN-10: 0-06-114996-9

Printed in Spain
First Printing, 2007

Acknowledgments
I would like to take this opportunity to thank architect Martin Despang and his colleague Jamison Burt for
their help, without which this book would not have been possible, and would undoubtedly have had half
the pages (and maybe not the best half). I would also like to thank photographer Wade Zimmerman and,
not least, all the architects and other photographers included in the book for their help and trust in
carrying out a project such as this one.

Contents

Introduction

The supermarket we choose for our weekly shopping is perhaps closer to the supermarket of the future than is first apparent. The fact that the Austrian chain MPreis can advertise itself as "The Seriously Sexy Supermarket," a slogan more appropriate for a chain of stores selling high-quality lingerie or even state-of-the-art MP3 players, is proof that the tastes and demands of today's consumer are different from those of even our own parents. The change is obviously for the better, since progress, like time, moves in only one direction: forward. The old, traditional supermarkets—windowless, neutral spaces separated from the outside by parking lots and cold (literally, since the low temperatures force customers to move quickly through the aisles in less time)—are being ditched in favor of newer, more comfortable designs.

Contemporary supermarkets are no longer merely impersonal spaces that display food and cleaning products on miles of shelving lit by deliberately inhuman lighting. While supermarket architecture in urban centers, with certain notable exceptions (some of which are featured in this book), has succumbed to a uniform and conservative inertia, stores located in smaller towns have been the perfect testing ground for architects around the world to carry out their most daring experiments in modern commercial architecture.

The-North-American-architect-Jordan-Mozer-succeeded-at-visually-presenting-one-of-the-problems-of-traditional-supermarket-architecture-and-design. This problem is the lack of punctuation marks, of signs that mark the divisions between the different sections of the supermarket. Preferably, signs that are of more use than the tiny ones that hang precariously from the ceiling and that are actually more difficult to locate than our favorite brand of cereal.

Obviously, other problems arise, not least the attachment of supermarket chains to the distinctive aspects of their brand image and a rigid internal structure from which, on only rare occasions, the architect been allowed to deviate. This is why the architects of several of the supermarkets featured in this book have chosen not to pay attention to the interiors, which offered nothing new, but instead to focus on the exteriors, where the supermarket can fulfill its potential for innovation. Still, almost more important than that which can be seen is that which cannot: an intention to carry something out, which in the end may prove impossible because of the client's reluctance. That, however, is the subject of another book.

Selfridges Foodhall

Architect	Future Systems
Location	Manchester, UK
Photograph	© Richard Davies

There are two ways to go about conceiving a supermarket: as a simple shopping mall dedicated to high-speed shopping, without too much emphasis on the design and selling of standardized prepared foods, or as a "social" center more akin to the old marketplaces, a place to stroll through while looking at, tasting, and, of course, buying the different foods and prepared meals. This was Future Systems's philosophy when designing the three supermarkets for Selfridges, of which the one in Manchester is without doubt the most representative, exemplifying the idea from which the entire project grew.

The supermarket's design and that of the food display stands is based on the image of the splash from a drop of water. The food is located on these stands, forming small mountains. Both the food shelves and the stands and freezers for the frozen food have a pseudo-sculptural shape that helps to create very specific circulation routes for the customers.

The plastic-look finishes and shiny details enhance the colors of the food, which are the customer perceives as being fresh and natural. On display around the nucleus of the supermarket hundreds of products have been apparently randomly but strikingly arranged, imbuing the space an almost artistic value. The radial arrangement of the lights rounds off this futuristic sensation, which hits the customer at first glance. The aim—for the customer to look, wander, chat with the shop assistants and taste, smell, and admire the product before buying it—has very obviously been achieved here.

The curved display stands in the supermarket give it a futuristic aesthetic that alludes to design in the 1960s. The lighting in the space has been arranged to enhance the curved elements in the shopping center.

RED WINE

WI

A unique display system for the wines and spirits, which fills one of the curved walls, transforms them into one of the supermarket's decorative elements.

Spar
Hohenems

Architect	**Arno Bereiter**
Location	**Hohenems, Austria**
Photograph	**© Arno Bereiter**

Arno Bereiter's Spar supermarket in Hohenems, a small town of fewer than 15,000 inhabitants in the heart of the Rhine Valley, is a perfect example of how a commercial building can be adapted without disturbing its surroundings. In this case, the building's roof, its "fifth façade," in the words of Arno Bereiter himself, has been designed to match the scale of the neighborhood. Hohenems is a mountain town, and so the supermarket can be seen not only from ground level but also from above by simply walking a few minutes up the mountain, which is not normally the case with most buildings. Perhaps because of this, Arno Bereiter proposed that the Spar chain plant a lawn on the roof; unfortunately, the idea was rejected, even though it could have given the building a highly novel dimension.

The supermarket is almost completely surrounded by the parking lot (only one of its four façades does not face the parking lot). This allows the enormous metal front awning that surrounds practically the entire building to act as a guide for visitors, showing them the way to the entrance. The foundations, main walls, and columns of the building are made of cement, and the main roof has been made with wooden laminates. The façade and the front awning are made of steel and perforated aluminum. The result is a building that integrates perfectly with its surroundings, minimizing its presence-but not sacrificing some interesting architectural details. The treatment of the roof as a "fifth façade," a concept that is virtually unheard-of in buildings located at ground level, lends originality to the project and makes the supermarket deserving of a closer look from the customer.

A metal laminate more than six feet wide surrounds the building's perimeter and guides the customer toward the entrance, making it the focus of everyone's gaze.

The idea to create a lawn on the roof, which was eventually
rejected, would have allowed the building to integrate more
subtly with its surroundings, camouflaging it and giving it
a radically different personality.

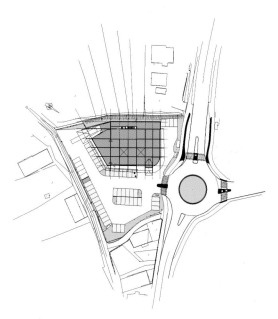

Site plan

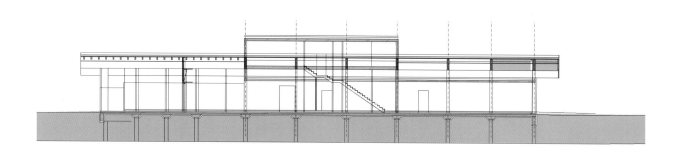

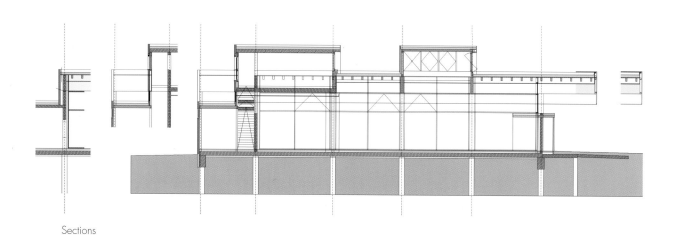

Sections

Sketch

Interspar
Graz

Architect	ATP — Achammer-Tritthart & Partner
Location	Graz, Austria
Photograph	© Angelo Kaunat

In 1998, the supermarket chain Spar successfully completed the renovation of its brand image, which was aimed at challenging the stiff competition from the other big chains and the new types of food stores. At that time, Interspar had been negotiating for years with the architectural firm ATP for the design and construction of a new supermarket, in the Austrian town of Graz, that would put this new brand image into practice. The main difficulty with the commission was building this commercial center in practically record time: no more than a year. ATP was responsible for all architectural and engineering aspects and planned and built the new supermarket within the time frame stipulated. (Work began in August 1998 and finished in the same month the following year; the supermarket opened its doors to the public just a month later.)

The supermarket, which stands on 205,000 square feet of land and has a total surface area of almost 860,000 square feet, cost 9.67 million Euros. In the entrance, a red panel several feet high and featuring the brand's logo welcomes the customer or attracts attention from a distance. The panel, therefore, does not just have a decorative effect but also acts as a beacon, allowing the passerby to visually locate the supermarket immediately. A second striking element of this supermarket is the roof, which juts out for several feet from the vertical face of the facade, creating a sheltered area that protects customers from the rain or the sun. A strip of windows beneath the roof surrounds the building, flooding the interior spaces with natural light.

Lights in the upper part of a panel that marks the entrance to the supermarket are protected from the rain by a small canopy. These lights illuminate the chain's logo.

The vertical column at the entrance to the parking lot and the
horizontal illuminated panel on the supermarket's roof reinforce the
brand's image and allow it to be seen from far away.

Dean & DeLuca

Architect	**Graphics & Designing**
Location	**Tokyo, Japan**
Photograph	**© Nobuko Ohara**

Dean & DeLuca, a high-quality chain of supermarkets has been offering a gourmet clientele exceptional food and products for 20 years. Of the five stores that the chain has in Japan (the chain has opened only one other supermarket outside the US, in Taipei, Taiwan), perhaps the most striking from the point of view of its design and architecture is the one located in the Shinagawa district, one of the fastest-growing in Tokyo and where one of the city's main bullet-train stations, Shinagawa Station, is located. In fact, the area is the third in the city in terms of numbers of skyscrapers, and this says a lot about its economic power and potential for growth. It was therefore just a matter of time before Dean & DeLuca chose to open one of its supermarkets here, following in the footsteps of various well-known companies that have moved their central offices to Shinagawa (among them such giants as Sony, Canon, Panasonic, Japan Airlines, and Mitsubishi Heavy Industries).

The Dean & DeLuca supermarket in Shinagawa includes not only the supermarket itself, but also a cafeteria and a newspaper kiosk. The interior design, which is defined by pure lines, soft lighting, and cold colors, allows the colors of the food, rather than the purely decorative details, to become the main attraction. Although the supermarket has maintained the look that Dean & DeLuca follows in the US, some details have been adapted to the Japanese aesthetic. On the ceiling, the pipes and other technical equipment have been left exposed as a decorative element whose coarseness and industrial appearance contrasts with the minimalist and elegant decorative elements, shelves, and display stands in the store.

The supermarket connects directly to Shinagawa Station, allowing customers to head directly for the store without having to go into the street. The fact that the supermarket is connected to the train station also allows residents from other areas of the city to come directly to the supermarket without having to negotiate a long walk around the neighborhood to find the store.

Sketch

The aesthetic of the Dean & DeLuca supermarkets is that of small
food shops from the 1930s and '40s, although the interior design is
completely contemporary.

The aesthetic and interior designs of Dean & DeLuca supermarkets is closer to that of small delicatessens than large supermarket chains.

Concept design sketch

Concept design sketch

DEAN & DELUCA

ICED DRINKS

	MEDIUM	LARGE	
	320	370	CHAI
COFFEE	350	390	CHOC
LATTE	350	400	NEW
CAPPUCCINO	360	410	FRA
MOCHA LATTE	370	410	ITA
REDEYE		370	FR
AMERICANO	320	370	FR
ESPRESSO	SINGLE 260 DOUBLE 320		F

SYRUP FLAVORS : VANILLA, CAR

HOT DRINKS

	SMALL	MEDIUM	LARGE	
HOUSE BLEND	260	300	340	
LATTE	300	350	390	
CAPPUCCINO	300	350	390	
MOCHA LATTE	320	370	410	
CAFE AU LAIT	300	350	390	
	320	370	420	

TEA			
CHAI TEA LATTE	320	370	340
HOT CHOCOLATE	340	380	420
STEAMER	300	350	390
HOT APPLE CIDER	300	340	380
	300	340	380

WHIPPED CREAM   SHOT +50

ESPRESSO   SHOT +50

World of Food

Architect	Kinnersley Kent Design
Location	Birmingham, UK
Photograph	© Carlos Dominguez

House of Fraser, founded in 1849, is the leading chain of designer-brand shopping malls in Great Britain, with more than 60 stores throughout the country, although not all operate under the name House of Fraser. For the center in Birmingham, Kinnersley Kent Design was commissioned to design the interior, the brand identity, and the packaging for more than 300 different product lines. The aim was to position House of Fraser products as top-of-the-line merchandise, and this was achieved by way of a global design that enhanced the brand's creative leadership and focused on a "culinary concept" of returning the simple pleasure of cooking with high-quality products to the spotlight.

The so-called World of Food Islands are located in the center of the space, around which are the basic ingredients of a host of gastronomic delights from around the world, all of which are sold in the supermarket. Each of the islands represents a different part of the world (Europe, India, Southeast Asia) and offers the choice of either buying or tasting typical dishes from that area or buying the ingredients to cook these dishes at home. The different spaces situated on the exterior perimeter of the supermarket are treated as individual shops in order to conserve their individuality and to help create a feeling of diversity and warmth. The wine store also offers customers the possibility of tasting wines that they may then decide to buy.

Besides the interior design, the packaging design and that of all the graphic elements in the supermarket have been conceived as a single integral piece. This is why people who work in the food-production process have been used as models, each of them representing a different geographical area. Images of these workers have been used to decorate the idyllic exteriors. The models were chosen because of their "authentic" look, which helps to provide a natural and fresh atmosphere.

The redesign of the supermarket extends to the graphic elements of
the products on display, such as the price tags and the type
used on them. A study of the colors used rounds off the redesign
of the graphics.

WORLD of FOOD
HOUSE OF FRASER

KORMA
Indian Curry Paste

WORLD of FOOD
HOUSE OF FRASER

GARLIC
flavoured Olive Oil

WHITE WINE
VINEGAR
with Chillies

THAI
flavoured Olive Oil

WHITE WINE
VINEGAR
with Raspberries

WORLD of FOOD
HOUSE OF FRASER

WORLD of FOOD
HOUSE OF FRASER

An elegant but calculatedly cold ambience places the supermarket in the higher-range bracket. The use of cold colors, such as white and all its variants (mainly marble), accentuates this effect.

Interspar
Rum

Architect	**ATP – Achammer-Tritthart & Partner**
Location	**Rum, Austria**
Photograph	**© Günter R. Wett**

Rum, in Austria, plays host to the first example of the Interspar chain of supermarkets. When ATP received the commission to redesign it, three different options were put forward that would "allow the space to rise from the ashes." After all suggested options had been studied, the new Interspar finally became a large, simple, and luminous space rising 28 feet above ground level, framed by a spectacular aluminum roof and an open parking lot with a lightweight structure. From the inside of the supermarket, and specifically at the north facade, the parking lot can be seen through an imposing window that provides the store with as much light as any other contemporary supermarket, where most windows are covered so that customers are not distracted by what is happening outside. In the opposite sense, all products on display inside, as well as the layout of the spaces, can be seen from the supermarket's parking lot.

Inside of the supermarket, the ceiling suggests lightness and luminosity. The 32,300 square-foot space has just five Y-shaped columns, formed from 108-foot-long aluminum beams, that support the structure. These beams widen as they rise.

The Interspar supermarket in Rum also stands out for being the first to use firplamella, panels reinforced with high-strength fibers developed as part of the US space program. The areas of these panels that bear the most tension have been reinforced with carbon fibers, resulting in a 25 percent reduction in the thickness of the paneling and increased spacing between the supports.

Through the supermarket's large windows customers can admire the impressive views of the surrounding mountains.

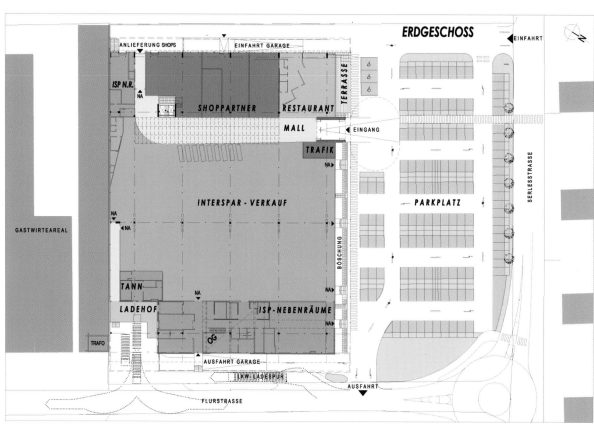

ERDGESCHOSS

EINFAHRT

ANLIEFERUNG SHOPS   EINFAHRT GARAGE

ISP N.R.

SHOPPARTNER   RESTAURANT   TERRASSE

MALL   EINGANG

TRAFIK

INTERSPAR - VERKAUF   PARKPLATZ   SERLESSTRASSE

BÖSCHUNG

GASTWIRTEAREAL

TANN

LADEHOF   ISP-NEBENRÄUME

TRAFO

OG

AUSFAHRT GARAGE

LKW LADESPUR

AUSFAHRT

FLURSTRASSE

Floor plan

Through the large supermarket windows customers can admire the
impressive views of the surrounding mountains.

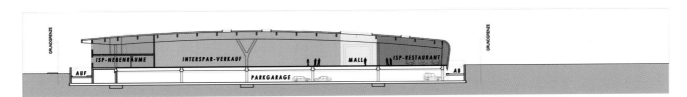

Longitudinal section

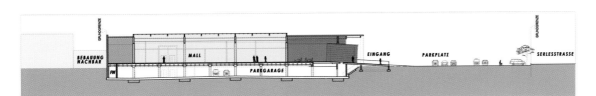

Cross section

At night, the supermarket's illuminated roof acts as a crown of light
that accentuates the length of the mall and acts as an advertisement
for customers.

The roof panels, called firplamella, represent a radical technical
advance that allows highly innovative architectural
solutions.

MPreis Sillian

Architect	**Machné Architekten**
Location	**Sillian, Austria**
Photograph	**© Paul Ott, Graz**

The unusual shape of the plot of land where this MPreis supermarket was to be built, in the small Tyrolean town of Sillian, allowed for an entirely innovative configuration of an interior space measuring 200 feet long and barely 40 feet wide—quite a lot smaller than usual for a building of this type. To overcome these potentially problematic dimensions, the interior was designed with only two aisles, one for each direction. This allows the customer to move around the supermarket from the entrance to the end and back toward the checkout at the exit, avoiding endlessly wandering around mazes of badly organized aisles.

The lateral walls of the building are 20 feet high, and the front and back walls are made of glass. The roof houses all the usual installations and allows rainwater to run off directly into a tank located at the back of the supermarket.

The exterior wall that faces east, and thus receives the greatest amount of sunlight throughout the day, has been resurfaced with a neat mesh of small boards that, over time, will acquire an attractive patina from the effects of light and rain. A narrow window that separates the walls from the ceiling allows sunlight to flood the interior space. The food on the display shelves receives direct sunlight, giving it a more colorful appearance, which is uncommon in supermarkets, where a deliberately neutral and cold artificial light is normally used to display the products. The MPreis supermarket in Sillian has therefore developed its own character, setting it apart from conventional urban supermarkets.

The elongated shape of the building in which this supermarket is located allows for a completely logical organization of the product displays. Customers have just two routes: one going forward and the other backward.

The building's concave roof gives the building personality, although it also has an eminently practical function: to allow rain to drain off the back section of the supermarket.

The wooden floors and the diffuse interior lighting give the
supermarket warmth. The large windows make the most
of the natural light.

Neighborhood Grocery Center

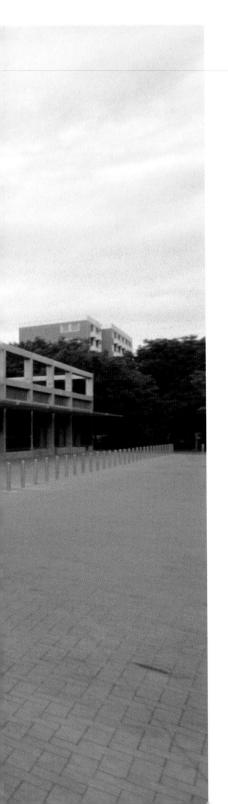

Architect	**Despang Architekten**
Location	**Hannover, Germany**
Photograph	**© Olaf Baumann**

A limited budget of 650 dollars per square meter was enough for Despang Architekten to refurbish an old public property and transform it into a shopping mall capable of competing on an equal footing with the large, modern supermarket chains. The original building was occupied in the 1960s by small local businesses, followed by various supermarket chains. These also eventually abandoned the space in search of ones adapted to their logistical and commercial needs.

In close collaboration with the town-planning department of Hannover's town council, Despang Architekten decided to focus on an architectural plan that would meet the commercial needs of the neighborhood and move away from the standard designs of the large chains of urban shopping malls. A spectacular frame of cement beams organizes the different interior spaces of the mall, giving it a strong character.

On completion of the renovation, the response from the residents, who had been insistent in their requests to the Hannover town council to restore the old shopping mall, was incredibly positive. The new space allows locals to do their "heavy" shopping a stone's throw from home. This, in turn, encourages them to use public transportation when accessing the town center to do their "lighter" shopping. The family car, therefore, is reserved exclusively for trips out of town. Having a nearby supermarket allows neighborhood residents to plan their meals and the corresponding shopping lists, as people used to: on a day-to-day basis, rather than a weekly one, returning the family and its needs to the fore.

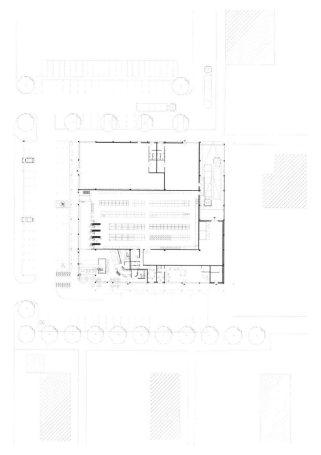

Site plan

Location map

The cement beams also serve as improvised, informal
seating, reinforcing the vision of the space as a social meeting place,
and not just a shopping mall.

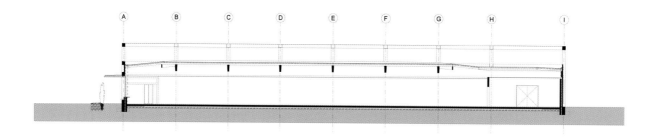

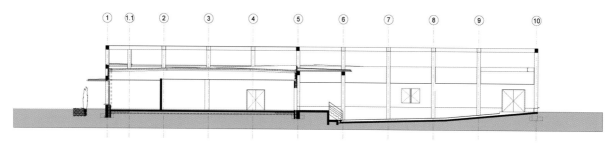

Logitudinal sections

The shopping carts are stored outside in a corral. Their bold color
allows customers to locate them immediately.

The supermarket's colorful logo forms a striking contrast with the cement beams that surround it. The aim is to attract the attention of passersby.

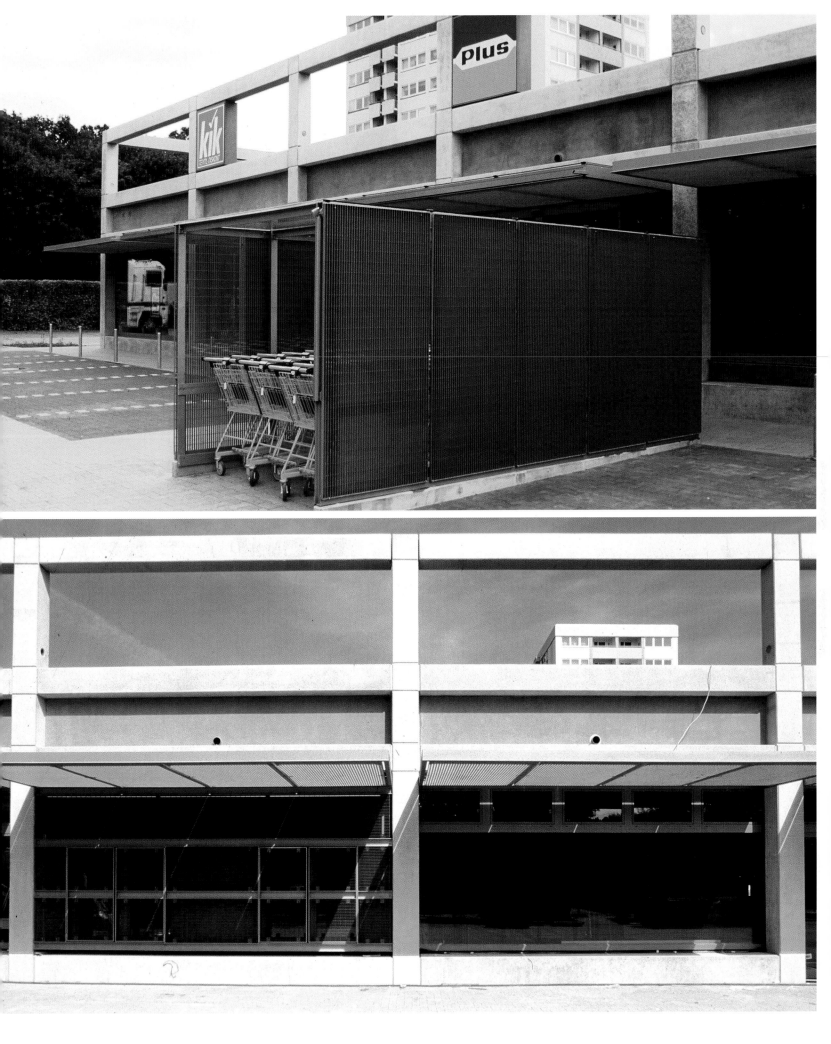

Santa Caterina Market

Architect	**EMBT – Enric Miralles & Benedetta Tagliabue**
Location	**Barcelona, Spain**
Photograph	**© Duccio Malagamba**

Ciutat Vella, Barcelona's old central district, is a microcity in itself. Modern town planning has been unable to address and find solutions to the problems inherent in this type of neighborhood, and a bizarre mix of old and new emerges. The resulting hybrids are at times dubious and on occasion magnificent. An example of the latter is without a doubt the renovation of the emblematic Santa Caterina Market.

The restoration of this traditional market comprises five separate sections: the underground parking, the automatic garbage-collection center, the organization of the archaeological remains of the Santa Caterina convent, the shopping area, and the apartment buildings. The total built-up surface area is 225,300 square feet, on a plot of almost 23,000 square feet. After being renovated, the market, together with the nearby Carders Street, is the center of urban renovation in Barcelona's latest fashionable neighborhood.

Three of the original market façades have been preserved and unified by the building's roof. The central area of the original market has been demolished, and the original perimeter has been reconstructed. The market's distinctive features are the original wooden supports, which, together with the structure of pillars and metal girders, hold up the wooden roof.

The design of the roof's ceramic surface is not, as some have wrongly pointed out, a tribute to Gaudí. It pays homage to the colorful array of fruits and vegetables typically found in Mediterranean markets, of which the Santa Caterina Market is certainly a superb example.

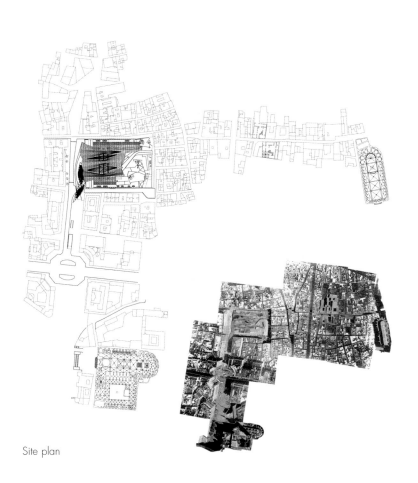

Site plan

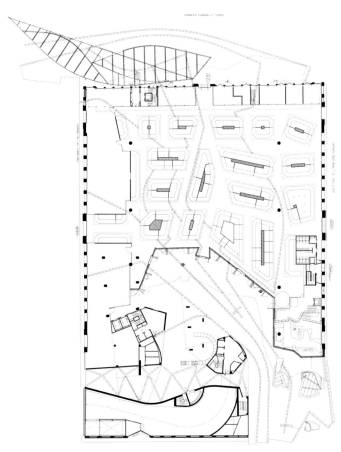

Floor plan

Front elevation of old Santa Caterina Market

Front elevation of new Santa Caterina Market

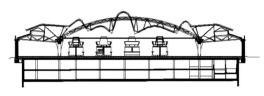

Section

Although it is the front facade that is spoken about most, the back facade, shown here, is as spectacular or more so than the front, thanks to the baroque wooden support beams.

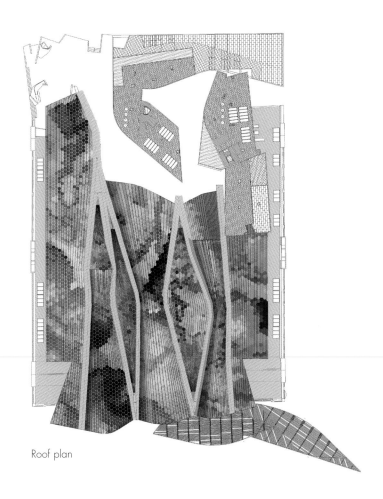

Roof plan

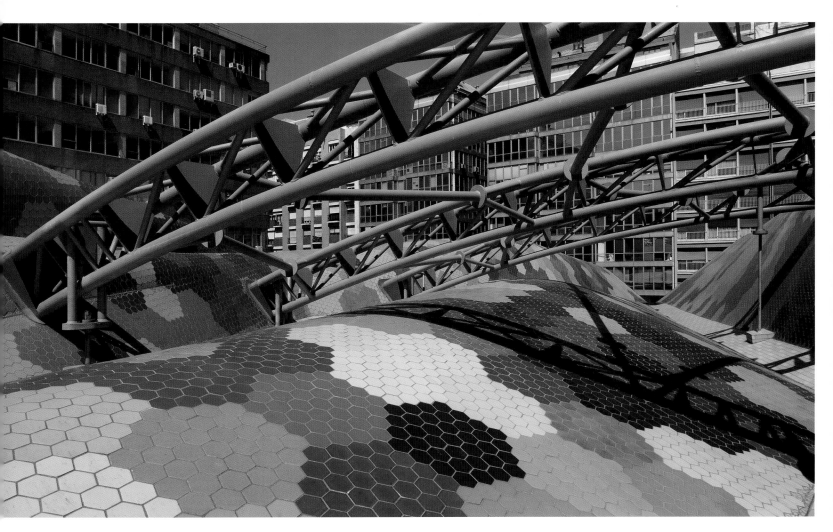

Shopping Center
Interspar

Architect	ATP — Achammer-Tritthart & Partner
Location	Vienna, Austria
Photograph	© Margherita Spiluttini

In 1999 the architectural firm ATP won the competition for the construction of a Spar supermarket in Vienna. The space where the new center would be built had been bought by Spar, which a short time before was the Pam-Pam Group. The Interspar Shopping Center had to incorporate all the elements of the brand's redesigned corporate image, which had been carried out the previous year by the same studio. The center was also the first to be built in accordance with the new design restrictions, in the center of a densely populated city.

At the heart of the new shopping mall we find the Interspar supermarket, which occupies a surface area of 37,000 square feet and contains all the comforts and usual services of modern shopping centers. The products are displayed in accordance with a new arrangement that is more coherent and user-friendly. The glass facade was conceived in response to the supermarket's location, on the corner of Sandleitengasse and Baumeistergasse streets, and to allow customers to enter the center from two different points. The facades, which are glazed, also reflect the surrounding urban landscape, adding another decorative element to the center and endowing the place with a clearly urban personality.

In the interior of the center, visual lightness and transparency are maintained, preventing the uncomfortable sensation of being in a completely closed space. Customers come across a central 33-foot-high atrium and 720 square feet of multimedia screens, which give the space a truly theatrical aura. On the ceiling are almost 11,000 square feet of cedar laminates, while the floor is composed of 37,000 square feet of natural stone pieces. Two elevators transport customers to the upper level of the mall, which offers a bird's-eye view of the lower level from the glass balconies.

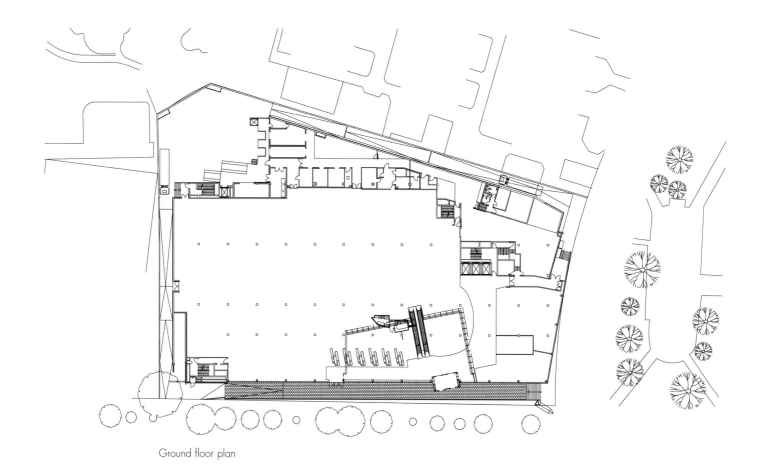

Ground floor plan

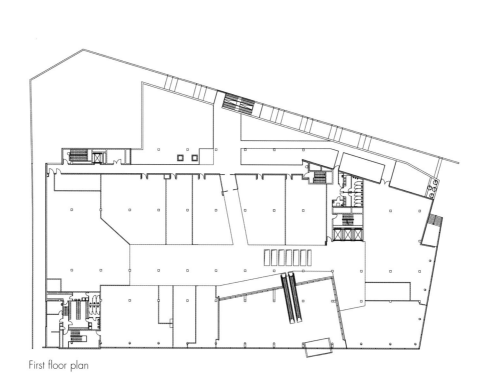

First floor plan

The luminous column with the brand's logo, normally found in Interspar supermarkets, can be seen both in the outside and the inside of the Interspar Sandleitengasse shopping center. Here, it is opposite the escalators that lead to the center's second floor.

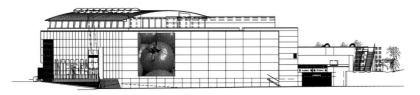

North elevation

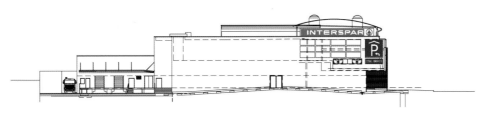

South elevation

East elevation

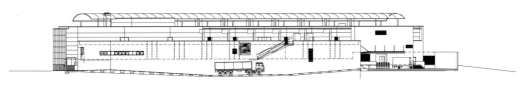

West elevation

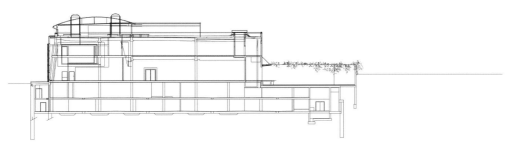

Cross section

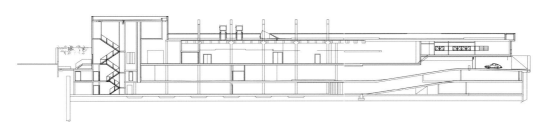

Longitudinal section

MPreis
Wattens

Architect	**DPA – Dominique Perrault Architecture**
Location	**Wattens, Austria**
Photograph	**© André Morin**

The second supermarket of the MPreis chain in Wattens, designed by Dominique Perrault, is characterized by its multifunctionality: The building, situated in the town center, not only houses the MPreis supermarket, but also contains a bank, a clothing store, a cafeteria, and the local police station. The structure stands above a parking garage, converting it into a floating structure with a visual lightness that is unusual for buildings of this type. Ramps sloping at different angles surround the garage and introduce natural light into the building's interior, while the surrounding moat is fitted with lighting that illuminates the supermarket's interior at night and reinforces the aforementioned lightness. The glass facade that partially surrounds the building enhances the natural light. However, the facade doesn't uniformly illuminate the interior space: Some sections have been covered by a curtain made from a metal alloy, fabricated by the company GKD – Gebr. Kufferauth AG, often used in Dominique Perrault's constructions. This allows more light to filter through the windows in some sections and less in others.

The trees outside have been planted strategically in the different modules of the building, giving it better integration with its surroundings. The aim, therefore, is to convert the supermarket into a social meeting place, rather than just a standard shopping mall, for local residents.

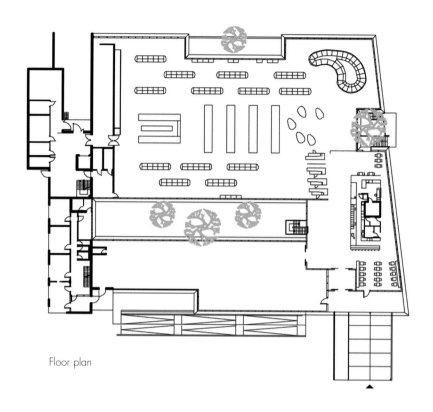

Floor plan

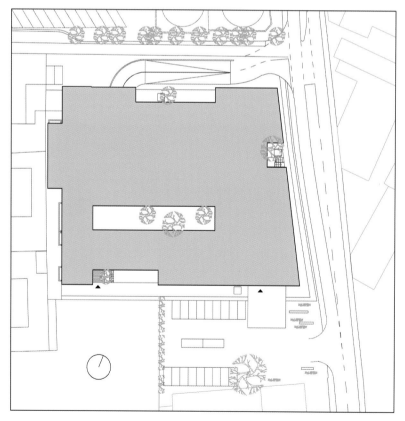

Site plan

The alloy curtain that can be seen on different parts of the building's facade, at different heights, allows the amount of light that enters through the windows to be filtered and regulated.

The artificial lighting, sunk into the building's ceiling, uniformly
illuminates the products on display, while the natural light provides
warmth and on sunny days enhances the colors of the food.

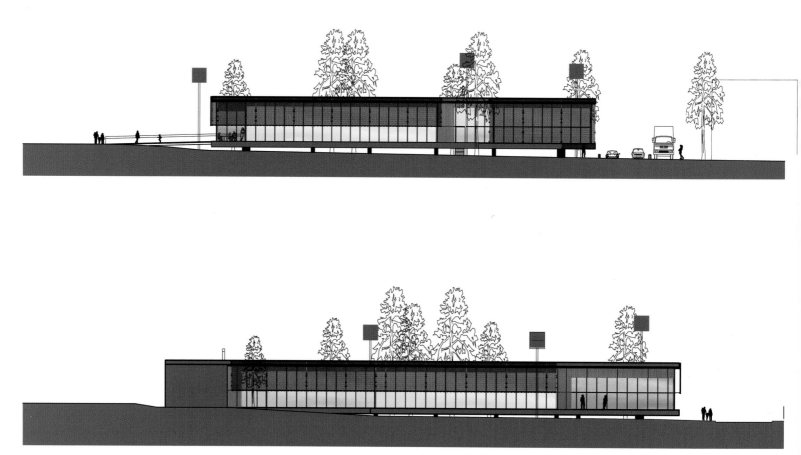

Elevations

The lights that illuminate the building's entry canopy have been placed in line with the supermarket's interior lighting, which together with the glass facade blurs the separation between exterior and interior.

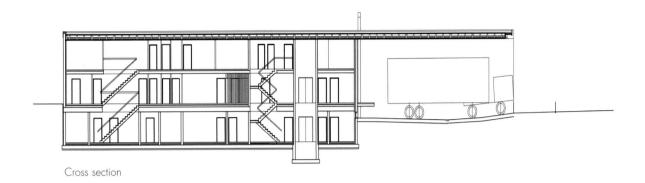

Cross section

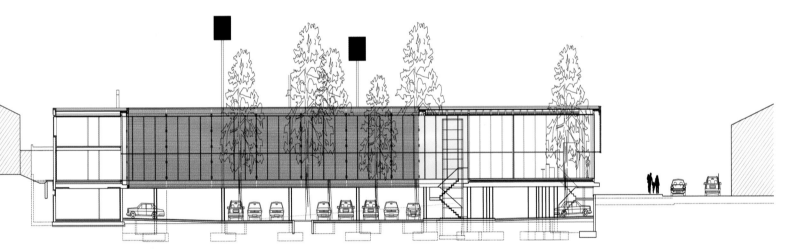

Longitudinal section

The trees that surround the building have been treated, from a design point of view, as another decorative, if not architectural, element. Without them, the project's starting point would possibly have been quite different.

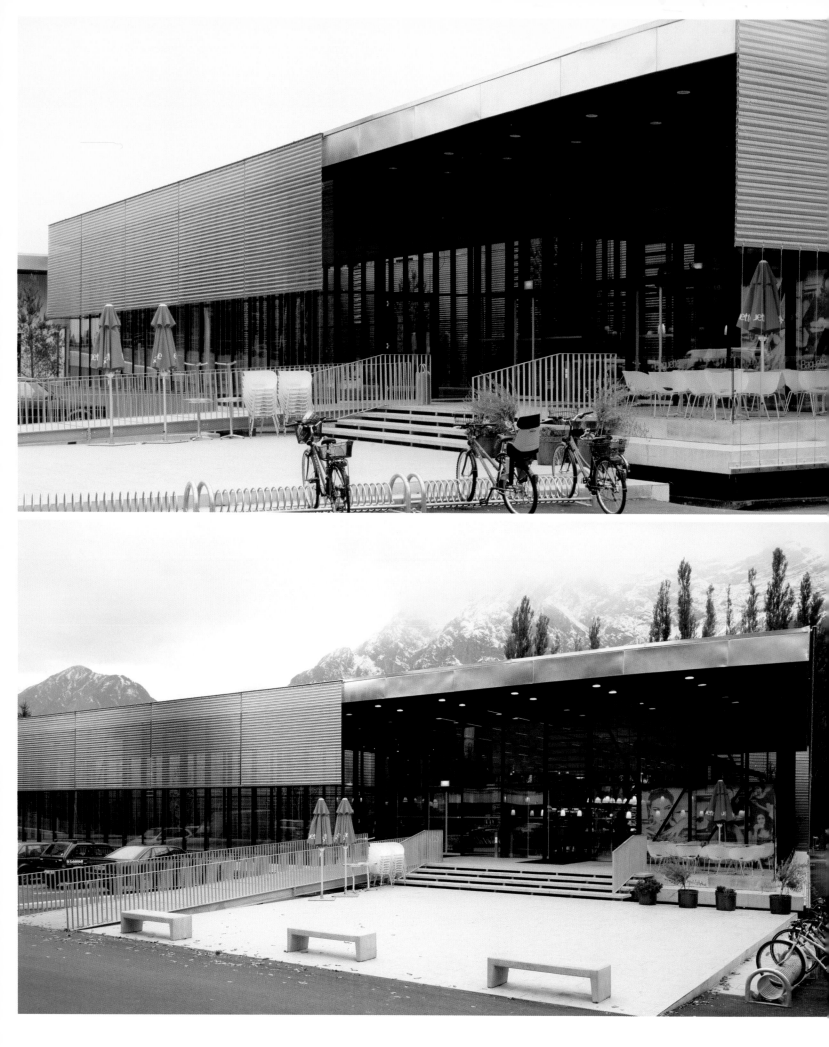

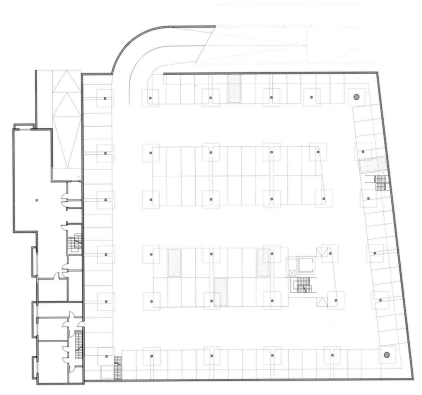

Park deck plan

A&P Dewy Meadow Village

Architect	**Create Architecture Planning & Design**
Location	**Basking Ridge, NJ, USA**
Photograph	**© Wade Zimmerman**

The problem Create was confronted with for this supermarket was the opposite of those of most other projects in this book: the need not to resort to clichés when designing the A&P supermarket in Basking Ridge, which includes an adjacent pharmacy. The center's architecture had to make reference to the area's history and convey a sense that the entire supermarket had been planned as a town square. To achieve this, the center was designed to reflect the architecture of A&P supermarkets from the early 1900s.

The problems became clear when trying to reconcile this "retro" architecture with modern antifire legislation by way of a steel superstructure that would imitate the wooden structures of more than a hundred years ago. Another obstacle came from the fact that both the supermarket and the annexed pharmacy are double the size of their twentieth-century predecessors. Obviously, the use of certain types of wood featured in many buildings from the early twentieth century is forbidden today, so Create had to look for alternatives. The use of such materials as steel, for example, offered certain advantages, such as better usage of space and a different, more logical positioning of the building's roof. The result was a dynamic front entry and checkout area, where the doghouse dormers allow additional light into the store.

Perhaps the most significant problem that Create had to deal with, however, was the regulations concerning the maximum size stipulated for this type of building. The number of square feet allowed for this type of construction was quite simply, not enough. The solution was to connect the pharmacy area of the store, which also sells durables and toiletries, to the main food hall, with a glass-enclosed breezeway. This solution created two buildings, which complied with local regulations and also allowed shoppers to travel between them in a fully enclosed, climate-controlled environment.

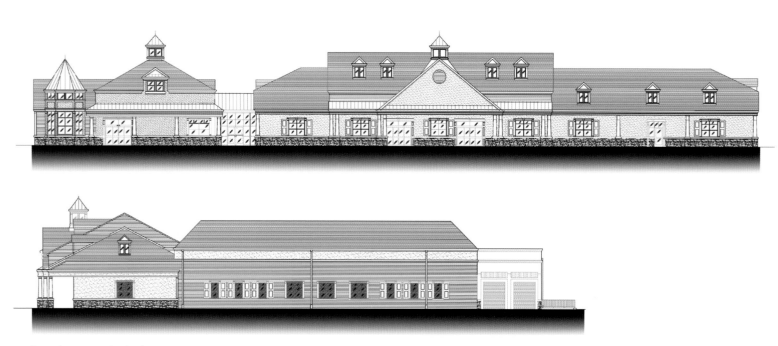

Front elevation and side elevation

The Basking Ridge supermarket is a true journey into the past, an homage to supermarkets from the turn of the twentieth century, and not, as could be thought at first glance, just an attempt at a retro style.

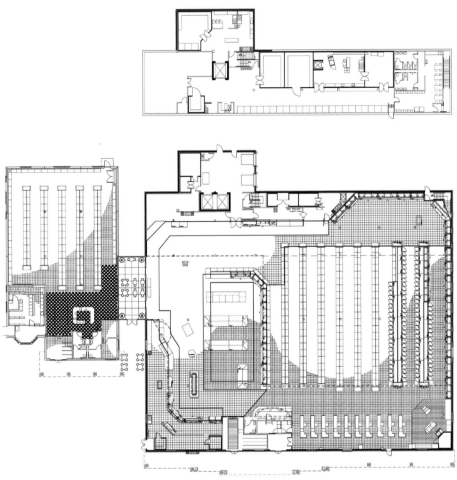

First floor plan and second floor plan

Marsh

Architect   Jordan Mozer
Location   Naperville, IL, USA
Photograph   © Doug Snower

Jordan Mozer's Marsh supermarket is probably one of the most perfect contemporary examples of how to redesign a commercial space intelligently and without giving in to the usual clichés. In fact, when John Turek, of Marsh supermarkets, phoned Jordan Mozer to ask him and his team to design a new prototype for the supermarket, what he was really looking for was ideas that parted from a preconceived format, far away from those of the large supermarket chains—ideas that were not just a twist on old standards but would break with the rules and create something completely new.

The center of the supermarket plays host to a colorful and cheerful marketplace of natural products and kiosks: a bar, a newspaper kiosk, a sushi restaurant, a nursery, and a pharmacy surrounded by small seats. This area is not just the geographical center, it also constitutes the shopping mall's social center.

The ceiling of this central marketplace rises to a height of 32 feet, while in the surrounding area the height descends to 13 feet. This exterior space has been divided according to the products sold in each area (delicatessen, cheeses, health, pets, wines, bakery, butcher shop, etc.), which are clearly indicated with signs have the look of main-street signs in cities in the United States. From the supermarket's center, customers can easily see the surrounding signs and can, therefore, walk from one specialized area to another by cutting through the central space or by walking around this exterior area and glancing at the various products available to them on the way.

On the wall that balances out the changing heights of the mall's ceiling are many windows that flood the space with natural light, reducing energy consumption and giving the space a warmer and more pleasant atmosphere.

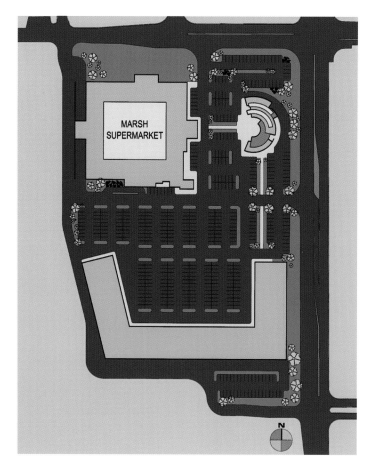

Park deck plan

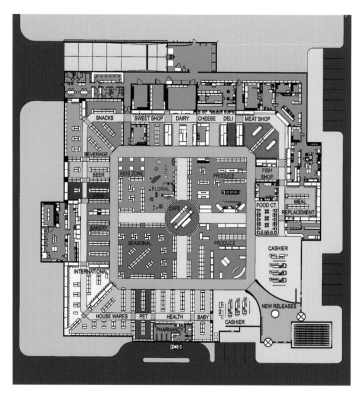

Floor plan

Design concept sketches

On the wall that balances out the changing heights of the center's ceiling, dozens of windows, which flood the space with natural light, have been put in place, allowing for significant energy savings and offering a much more pleasant, warmer atmosphere.

The salad lover is spoilt for choice here with half an isle dedicated
to an impressive selection of dressings and toppings.

The information terminal has come a long way from the booth
crowned by a question mark, which can be seen on the opposite
page, to today's design, which is much more simple.

Information terminal sketch

Design concept sketch

Design concept sketch

MPreis Wörgl

Architect	Tatanka Ideenvertriebsgesellschaft
Location	Wörgl, Austria
Photograph	© Paul Ott, Graz

The enormous cement structure of the MPreis supermarket in Wörgl, a small town with a population of no more than 8,500, contains five thick columns whose interiors hold stairs and elevators that allow customers to access the building's different levels without having to negotiate all the aisles. This energy-efficient building extracts the energy needed for levels 0 and 1 of the supermarket from water in the ground.

The supermarket's interior is kept warm by heaters installed in the building's main ceiling, which is made of cement and measures 28 inches thick in the middle and 14 inches at the sides. The roof is made of pieces of laminated wood, lined with XPS insulation panels.

An immense, concave solar panel covers the western facade, which has been adorned by the convex, metal roof of another supermarket in Innsbruck. A ramp leads from the supermarket's ground floor to the second floor. Inside, wide aisles and high ceilings provide a pleasant, open feeling, uncommon in urban supermarkets, in which space is normally much more restrictive.

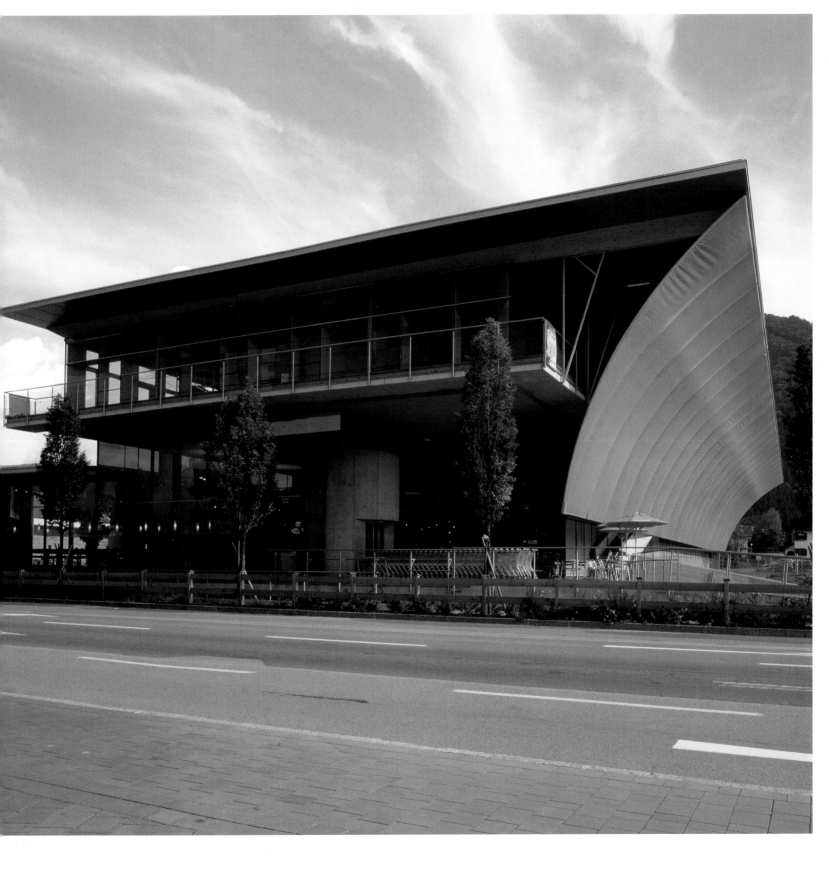

The curve of the supermarket's lateral facade, which completely covers the building's two extra stories, creates an unusual profile, more in keeping with avant-garde architecture than that of a commercial building.

By being partly raised on pillars, the supermarket acquires a
presence it would not have had it been constructed
at ground level.

Shoppers, who can access the building's interior directly from the
parking lot, can park their cars beneath the supermarket itself and
thus be protected from the rain and snow.

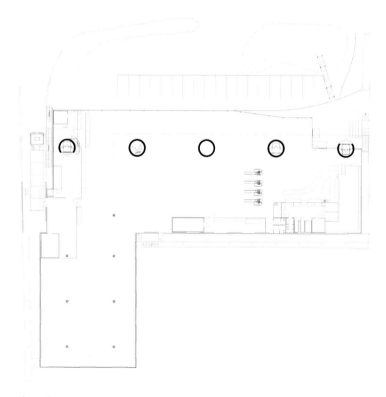

Floor plan

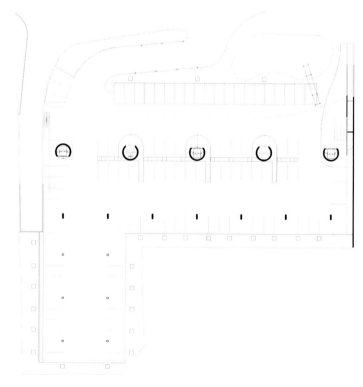

Park deck plan

A small 30 foot long ramp leads to the supermarket's first floor
and to a terrace where customers can sit at tables, rest, and
have a drink.

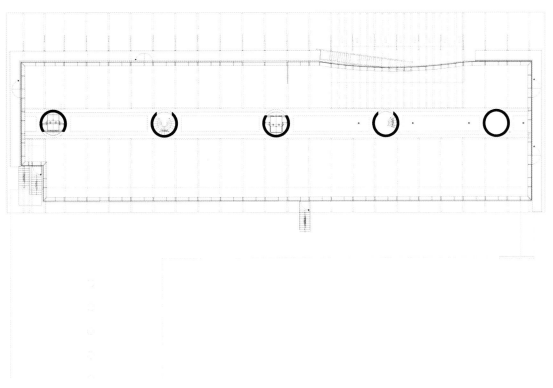

Upper floor plan

Hypercity

Architect   **JHP Design**
Location   **Mumbai, India**
Photograph   **© Sanjay Marathe Photography**

Barely 90 days after its opening, a million shoppers proved the success of the Hypercity supermarket, the first of its kind in India. Its 398,264 square foot surface area has been designed with the goal of offering the customer an experience that goes beyond that of simply doing the daily or weekly shopping. Hypercity also offers customers a 24-hour pharmacy, a bakery, two coffee shops, and express checkouts for speedy service. Sales during its first three months exceeded the owners' most optimistic forecasts by 40 percent.

Hypercity , the first supermarket of the K Raheja Corporation in India, offers the possibility of seeing what the India of the future will be like, from the point of view of its commercial potential. Inside the center, the customers can find a wide variety of food products available in the market, as well as products in areas such as multimedia, sports, books, toys, cleaning products, health and beauty, and so on. The JHP team, commissioned with the design of the space, decided to respect the color palette used by Luis Barragan for the brand's identity, which reflects both the optimism of a country on its way to becoming an economic and political power, as well as the bright, eye-catching colors that can been seen in the streets throughout the country.

In the words of Rak Wilkinson, joint managing director of JHP, "On opening day customers came in, looked around in awe, and then picked up their trolleys and shopped as if they had done it a thousand times before. The standards of consumer expectation are getting higher and higher in the Indian retail sector. If our work has taught us one key lesson, it is that nobody can ever know it all and that the ability to understand and adapt the store design to cultural diversity is an essential prerequisite for success."

JHP used local clay for the floor to achieve a contrast between darkness and light. The different spaces are clearly delineated, and the islands are sufficiently spacious to allow customers to pass each other without any pushing.

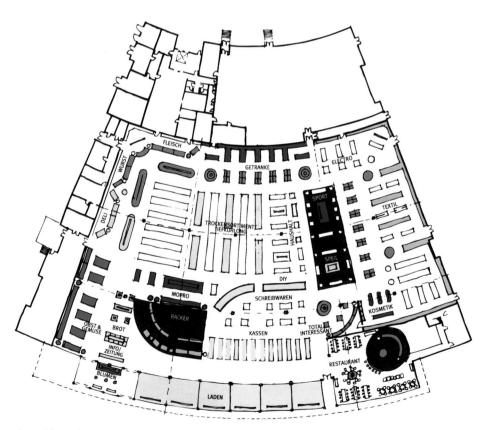

Ground floor plan

JHP Design used local clay for the floor, with the aim of achieving the desired contrast between light and dark. The different spaces of the supermarket are clearly delineated, and the islands are sufficiently spacious for customers to be able to circulate without bumping into each other.

The supermarket's aesthetics combine certain typically Indian elements, such as the colors and materials often used in the area, with other purely Western ones, like the wooden laminates of the dividing walls.

The color palette chosen for the interior can even be seen on the upper section of the display shelves. This is so that these colors can be seen from the upper floor.

The colors of the brand are commonplace in the clothes and on the streets of India, and this immediately increases the customer's sense of familiarity with the supermarket.

Qualicum Foods

Architect	Lind Design International
Location	Qualicum Beach, B.C. Canada
Photograph	© Gary Lind

Located in an upscale town center near Vancouver, Canada, Qualicum Foods forms part of a building divided into three different levels. The first two are the property of Qualicum Foods, while the third is occupied by leased shops, in the manner of a traditional shopping mall.

Curiously, the supermarket's interior design avoids all signs that the client would immediately associate with a conventional supermarket chain. The aisles are not laid out parallel to one another but instead form winding curves throughout the building, creating islands occupied by displays of food of all types. The exterior perimeter of the supermarket is reserved for the fresh or prepared-food counters. Across the shopping mall's width and length, certain decorative details associate the store with traditional outdoor marketplaces or the typical Mediterranean market: striped awnings and wooden display stands or carts similar to those used years ago on farms. The building's multiple pitched roofs reinforce this perception of the super-market as being more like a rural marketplace than a conventional urban supermarket. Architecturally, the building has a steel structure and masonry walls. The supermarket's logo on the front facade is visible from a distance, and it invites passersby—attracted by the unusual look, especially the roof framework—to enter.

The exterior aesthetics of the supermarket hint at a retro atmosphere,
associated, in terms of marketing, with natural "long-life" products.

In the supermarket's interior, the use of materials like wood
and of colors like orange, brown, and cream gives warmth
to the atmosphere.

The irregular arrangement of the products, which follows
no particular pattern but is seemingly random, reinforces the
sensation of being in an old village marketplace.

Interspar Linz

Architect	JHP Design
Location	Linz, Austria
Photograph	© Sarah Louise Ramsay

The fast-food culture does not exist in Austria. Food whose preparation has been hidden from view is considered to be suspect and clearly not recommended. In Interspar, the diverse range of shoppers, who vary from snack-grabbing office workers to Ladies Who Lunch, are encouraged to choose the freshest, most appetizing products from the market, give them to one of the supermarket chefs, and ask him to put a meal together that can be eaten there in the supermarket or taken away. The cooking is always on show for the consumer to see, and there is not a single step of the process that is hidden from view; even those that seem insignificant are clearly visible. The goal is to win the consumers' confidence in the brand and gain their loyalty by offering them in the supermarket the same treatment that they would receive in one of the city's best restaurants, and with equally good or superior food quality.

In Austria, the department store is also a rare phenomenon. In its place is an advanced hypermarket culture that pervades even the most upmarket malls. It is practically impossible to escape or live outside this hypermarket culture, and any attempt to opt for another type of solution will be met at first with resistance from the consumer. Therefore, to be commercially viable, supermarkets must respond to numerous shopping missions, desires, and mind-sets.

JHP received the commission to reinvent and give a different angle to the traditional concept of the fresh market, the food hall, and the restaurant in Austrian supermarkets. Or, more specifically, to design a completely new format for the new Plus City mall in Linz that would give meaning to a space selling everything from food to wines and spirits and clothes to cleaning products.

The Interspar in Linz, among others, received the Food & Supermarket Design of the Year Award in the 2005 Retail Interiors Award.

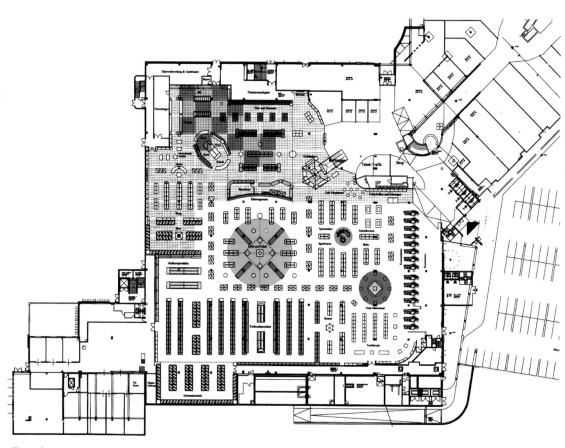

Floor plan

inter
mezzo

The dominant use of greens and reds creates a unique atmosphere
that gives the supermarket its distinctive personality.

The supermarket also has a kiosk selling the latest newspapers and
magazines and allows customers to read while they eat in the
supermarket's restaurant.

frischgemacht

Customers can easily see how the staff in the supermarket cook, store, and package the food that is found in the display stands.

Home Economist Market

Architect	**Little**
Location	**Charlotte, NC, USA**
Photograph	**© Jeffrey Clare**

How can you increase clientele by clearly repositioning your brand, without losing your traditional clientele? When the organic-foods store Home Economist Market decided to expand its business, it chose the architectural studio Little to re-plan the store in terms of its design and its architecture. First, Little carried out an exhaustive identification of Home Economist Market's distinctive "brand" elements to conserve them and thus provide both the old and the new clientele with totally intuitive decorative elements. These facilitate shopping, since customers do not have to spend too much time learning and remembering the new codes of the store. The graphic design team collaborated with architects, interior designers, and engineers to completely reinterpret the brand's distinctive elements without compromising their essence, so that all these elements would keep some kind of internal coherence that would be identifiable at first sight. Likewise, the signing system is also completely intuitive. When they enter the store, customers and visitors are greeted by murals by local artists that make reference to scenes or situations related to the production and consumption of fresh and natural organic food products.

Previous market research regarding the reform revealed that customers wanted a more relaxed and "natural" purchase, so design elements associated with natural materials and aesthetics were reinforced, giving the space greater warmth. To increase the sensation of spaciousness yet reduce the "strange" sensation of being in an unusually large space, the display areas were designed so that the customer can take in the entire store on entering. On passing through the doors of the supermarket, customers can easily see the space's four corners without any elements coming between them and these four points of reference.

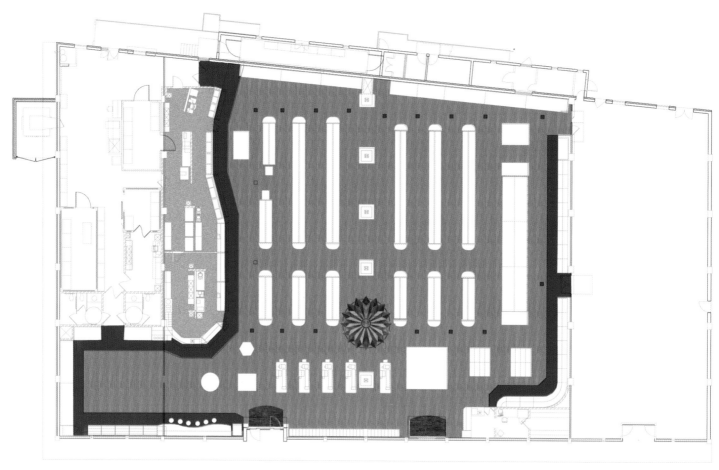

Floor plan

The use of materials like wood, which is warm and perceived by customers as "natural" and "traditional," contributes to the space's relaxed atmosphere, which generates a feeling of trust.

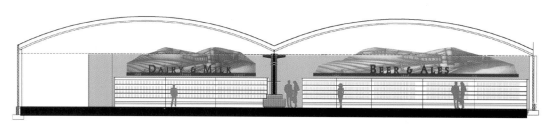

Elevation

A subtle use of color reinforces those parts of the store that are intended to have a particular personality and visually distinguishes them from other, adjacent zones.

MPreis Matrei

Architect	**Machné Architekten**
Location	**Matrei, Austria**
Photograph	**© Paul Ott, Graz**

The combination of both organic and purely architectural forms makes the MPreis supermarket in Matrei one of the most peculiar and original of all those included in this book. This split personality, halfway between the traditional and the contemporary, does not go unnoticed by customers and becomes the main feature, giving the store a striking personality.

A second detail worth mentioning is the supermarket's roof, which has been designed as the building's fifth "wall," since it can be easily seen by users of the skilift on the nearby slopes. In fact, this facade is the most visible of all the facades, which explains why it has received as much attention, from an aesthetic point of view, as any of the supermarket's other architectural features.

The building backs on to the adjacent highway, and, with the exception of a curve in the road from where the north facade is easily seen, it is almost invisible to the cars that whiz along this stretch of road. The building opens onto the village, thanks to large windows, that offer fantastic views of the stunning scenery.

In the supermarket's interior, the customer and visitor meeting points occur naturally where the aisles that provide the store's divisions cross, and where the best panoramic views of the scenery outside can be seen. A seating area and a bar in the supermarket also serve as a meeting and rest point for skiers after a day on the slopes.

The height of the display shelves, slightly higher than usual, does
not block the customers' view through the glass walls of the
surrounding scenery.

The building's roof is without doubt the main architectural attraction.
In the interior, the ceiling houses a lighting installation that goes
practically unnoticed by the shopper.

The building's roof, which juts out a few feet, like an awning,
provides an area of shade for customers waiting in the doorway.

The building's roof undulates and descends to ground level,
"brushing" the car park and delineating its perimeter.

As in all supermarkets of the MPreis chain, the cube with the brand's logo in a red background enjoys a privileged position, its aim being to be seen from far away by customers.

At night, the building seems to fuse with the mountains that surround it. The interior lights and those in the parking lot create a true visual spectacle that is further enhanced by the striking and sinuous supermarket roof.

Maxi Markt

Architect   **JHP Design**
Location   **Bruck, Austria**
Photograph   **© Sarah Louise Ramsay**

Designed as "the food world's answer to IKEA," JHP's Maxi Markt had to tackle a difficult problem: how to convert a massive space into a shopping mall on a "human" scale. The initial plans addressed two difficulties. First, the building had to adapt to its location in a remote and inaccessible location in Central Europe, which obliged locals to take full advantage of the few hours of good weather to do the weekly shopping. Second, the shopper had to be able to cover every one of the aisles in the supermarket quickly and without the sensation of being "remote-controlled" by the interior.

The building's neon-lit structure allows passersby to see the building from hundreds of feet away. This visual impact works not just from a distance but from close up as well, especially when the onlooker is facing the front facade. The brand's logo, which some consider to be "retro," has been preserved, and not just for aesthetic reasons (since "retro" has come back into fashion). Customers of the brand have shown that they are familiar with it, and can therefore quickly identify a Maxi Markt shopping mall in advertisements or any sort of commercial sign.

Shoppers are led around the store through areas called "very interesting zones." These may be special offers, tasting areas, or promotional events, which make every visit to a Maxi Markt a novel experience. The shop also includes products from outside the food sector, so some of the display spaces needed to be rethought. In addition, the owners stipulated that the space be capable of assimilating possible future extensions and commercial adaptations, depending on consumer interest.

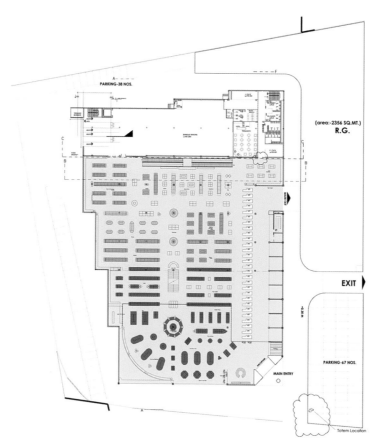

Ground floor plan

maxi markt

öffnungszeiten

mo – fr:
8:30 – 19:00
sa:
8:00 – 17·00

Large panels and posters illustrated with photographs cover the
enormous walls of this supermarket, helping to visually minimize its
size, and reducing it to a human scale.

In the wine and spirits section, the use of wooden boards reinforces
the feeling of being in a traditional wine cellar. The slate coloring
of the signs reinforces this impression.

The Maxi Markt supermarket makes no attempt to hide its true nature as a retail store, hence the arrangement of the light sources floods the space uniformly and enhances the colors of the products on display.

At night the eye-catching reddish lighting of the building's front
facade transforms the building into a focal point for all those passing
within a couple of hundred feet.

The brand's logo, framed by a red strip, leads the way for all the graphics and the lighting in the rest of the supermarket.

Uncle Giuseppes'

Architect	Lind Design International
Location	Smithtown, NY, USA
Photograph	© Gary Lind

Lind Design International was the firm chosen to design and construct an Italian-themed gourmet retail market in a space that, in the words of Gary Lind himself, was nothing more than "four bare walls." The location was the upper-middle class neighborhood of Smithtown, 50 miles from Manhattan. The owners of the space had decided to add a new level to their small but successful concept store, which would house a supermarket. Today, Uncle Giuseppes' has two more supermarkets in addition to the one in Smithtown: one in Port Washington and another in East Meadow.

The Uncle Giuseppes' in Smithtown is located in a commercial district, and surrounded by other supermarkets belonging to large chains. The distinctive feature of Uncle Giuseppe's is the quality of its products, which customers associate with a traditional taste and quality thanks to a carefully chosen design and aesthetics that use elements from classical Italian folklore and architecture. In keeping with this idea is the chain's very Italian slogan: "*Qui si mangia bene*" ("Here you eat well").

The steel-framed building with masonry walls was designed after thorough research was carried out by the Lind Design International team. The result is a spectacular and inviting space that repeatedly alludes to the iconography of traditional Italy (arches, columns, warm colors, tiles reminiscent of classical Roman terracotta, and allusions to ruins of Imperial Rome) and that had to be adjusted to a far smaller budget than the decoration would lead customers to believe. To accomplish this, standard materials were used and personalized by way of an intelligent use of interior illustration and design.

Right from the building's front facade, the supermarket evokes a strong mental association with typically Italian aesthetics and atmosphere. This is true as well of the typography used for the brand's logo.

Harris Teeter

Architect	**Little**
Location	**Charlotte, NC, USA**
Photograph	**© Jeffrey Clare, Tim Buchman**

Charlotte is the United States' twentieth largest city, so when designing the Harris Teeter supermarket, the Little studio decided to reflect the culture and innovative philosophy of a modern and highly eclectic city. This redesign included all the interior elements of the supermarket, from the shelves and product displays to the lighting, distance between the aisles, aisle distribution, and customer-circulation routes. The design borrows elements from other commercial spaces in the area where the supermarket is located, such as art galleries, banks, restaurants, and cinemas, allowing the supermarket to blend with its environment and avoid looking out of place as do so many city supermarkets.

Little used translucent materials like plastic and glass, a radical lighting design, and a soft color scheme to accentuate the space's feeling of size. The customer is spared the sensation of claustrophobia that is often caused by modern supermarkets, normally designed with cold, flat lighting and without windows (to prevent the customer from being distracted). The use of translucent materials allows customers to see the products from the street. The columns that previously stood in the store were preserved. Surfaced with semi-reflective materials that make the light rebound onto the surroundings, they were reconfigured as a decorative element. The walls and floors, however, were designed with almost no decoration at all, allowing them to go unnoticed, and thereby accentuating the signs and different graphic elements found scattered around the store.

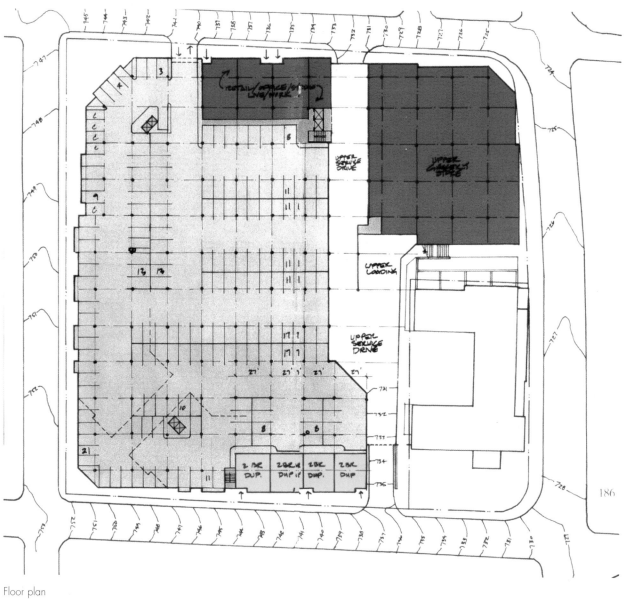

Floor plan

Powerful graphic elements mark and delineate the different zones this supermarket is divided into and allow customers to quickly locate the products for which they are looking.

This bird's-eye view highlights the sinuous line followed by the display stands situated to the right of the store and the imposing height of the central building, which has been visually lowered by way of an intelligent use of details and graphic panels.

A8ernA

Architect	NL Architects
Location	Koog aan de Zaan, Zaanstad, The Netherlands
Photograph	© Luuk Kramer

Koog aan de Zaan is a small Dutch town situated a stone's throw from Amsterdam. At the beginning of the 1970s, a highway was built that crosses the town. To be able to pass the Zaan River, which gives the town its name, the highway was raised using 23-foot-high columns. In the words of the architects from the NL studio, the highway became a "scar that split the town in half," ironically separating Church from State: On one side of the highway is the church and on the other, the town hall. Below the highway, where the columns rise from the ground, there was an empty space, a true "cathedral" of cement.

The A8ernA project sought to reconnect the two sides of the town, returning the unity they enjoyed before the construction of the highway. Some of the ideas presented by local residents, who wanted to convert this dead space once again into the town's center, were accepted: the construction of a supermarket, a parking lot for 120 cars, a florist, a pet shop, access to the river, a park, and the so-called graffiti gallery, along with a host of other architectural interventions and different services.

In this sense, the interest of the project lies not so much in the supermarket itself, clad in sheets of corrugated aluminum, but in its link with the surrounding space and services, which needed to fit into a site that was not at all easy to develop. The result is truly spectacular, an authentic example of how to revitalize an apparently useless urban space and how imagination and desire can enliven the grayest of urban spaces, turning defects into virtues and points of unquestionable architectural interest.

The building that houses the supermarket has a second floor above
the supermarket. Customers can see part of the interior of the second
level from the supermarket entrance.

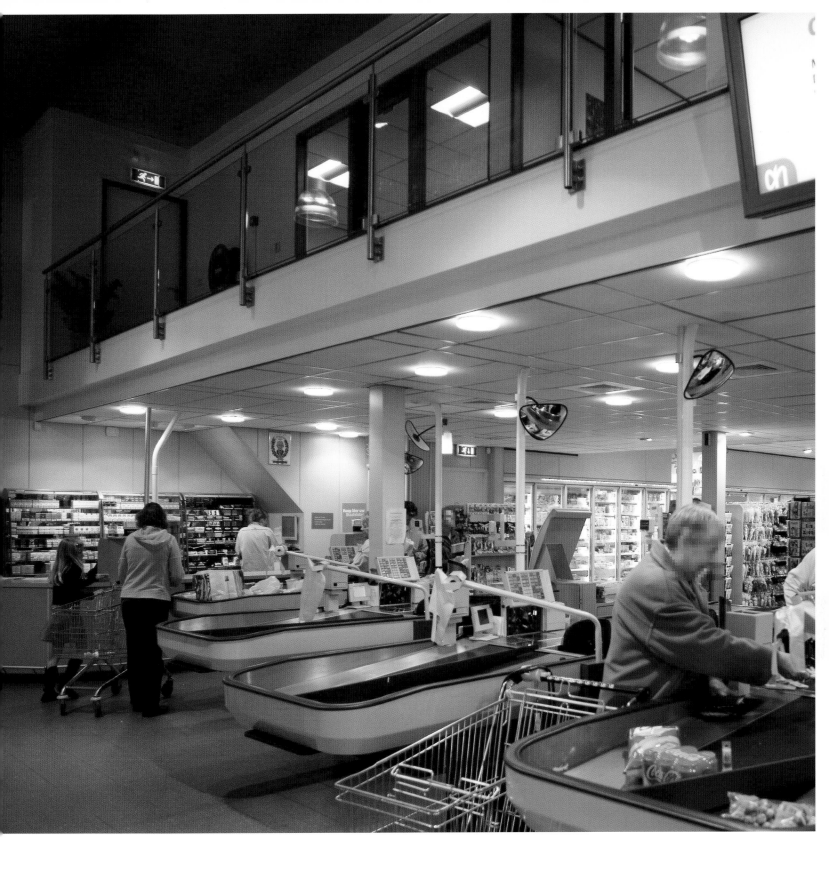

The warm colors and the ceiling, which is relatively low compared with what is usually seen in other supermarkets, give warmth to the space. The lighting is flat but uniform, meaning that no part of the store is lit more or less than another.

At the entrance to the supermarket, welcoming the customer, are four
pillars from the highway, which have been used as striking supports
for artistic work.

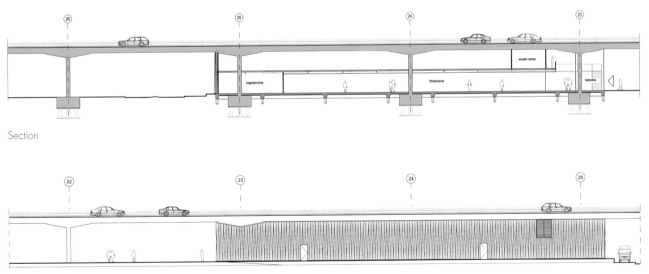

Section

Northeast elevation

Southwest elevation

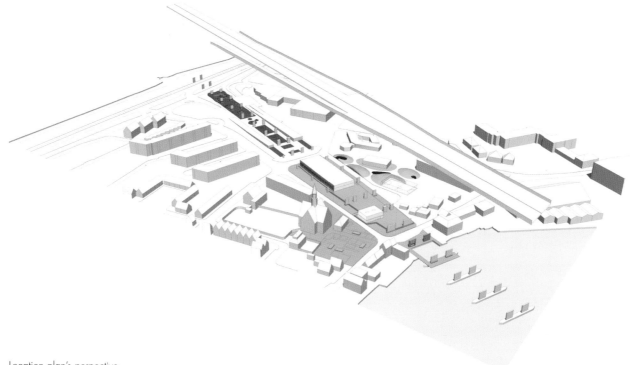

Location plan's perpective

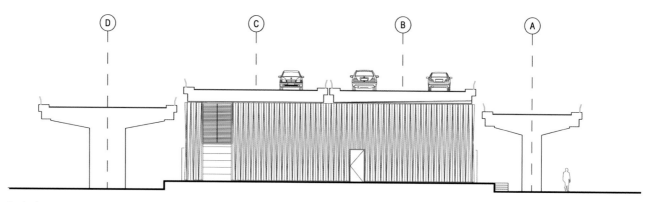

Back elevation

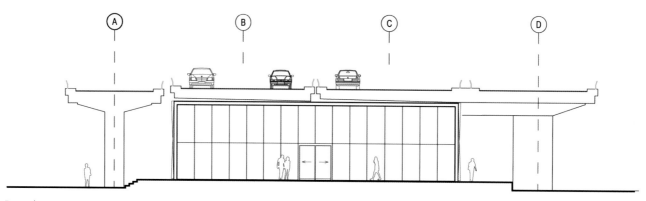

Front elevation

A highly appropriate architectural intervention has saved this from
being a dead space, which is so often the case for areas beneath
raised highways. The pillars that support the highway, far from being
an eyesore, have become the main attraction.

max.center

Architect	ATP – Achammer-Tritthart & Partner
Location	Wels, Austria
Photograph	© Alexander Koller

The max.center in Wels occupies the space previously occupied by a Maximarkt center and has received a Certificate of Merit as one of the best shopping centers in the world in the final of the International Council of Shopping Centers Award 2006. In fact, the max.center is the only Austrian entrant to receive an award in the contest.

The heart of the max.center is the new (and much bigger) supermarket Maximarkt. With a height in its central section of almost 39 feet, the new Maximarkt has been integrated with the structure of the max.center. The renovation was carried out with a new corporative design concept that can be applied to both new and old shopping malls alike. The architects and designers at ATP were chosen to rethink the Maximarkt concept, which would not only affect the "basic" characteristics, such as the size of the shop or the brand image, but also aspects like the recognition and value given by the customers, the entrance areas, or the advertising panels.

The design of the max.center, and therefore the new Maximarkt, is ecologically responsible. The building, for example, has glass panels that protect it from the rays of the sun on the south, east, and west facades, allowing the interior temperature to be lowered during the hotter months of the year. Furthermore, the roof has thermal insulation, which is thicker than was required by law, to avoid the accumulation of heat inside. A third aspect worthy of note is the use of LED lights at certain points on the facade, reducing the consumption of energy and also keeping maintenance to a minimum.

The max.center, which has been compared with a taco shell ("a colorful, generous, and spicy filling in a crispy casing"), has become an emblematic building for the western part of the city of Wels. Its imposing presence and avant-garde exterior dominate the landscape and attract all the attention.

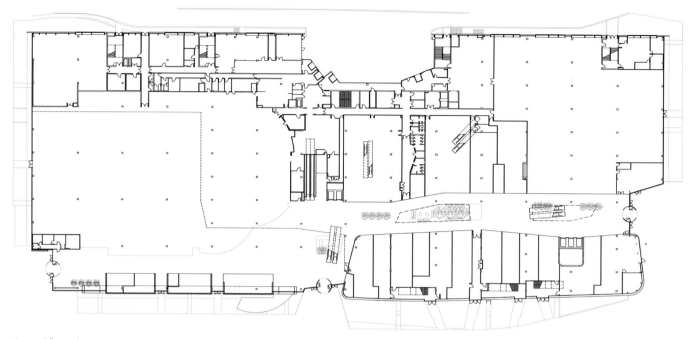

Ground floor plan

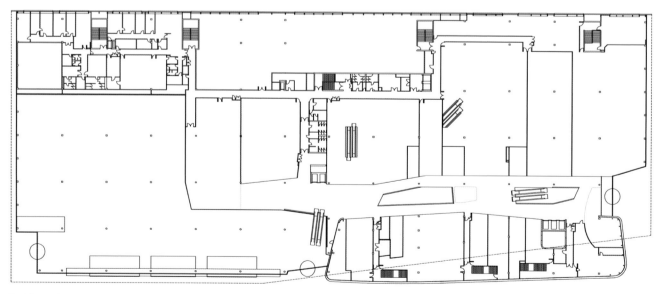

First floor plan

The original red logo of the old Maximarkt has been reinterpreted in the shape of a huge red framing element that symbolizes the transformation from the old supermarket to a larger and more modern shopping mall, which houses a new and completely reformed Maximarkt.

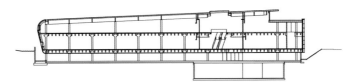

Cross section

Elevation

The lights that hang from the ceiling in the open central space of the
mall appear as fine drops of rain.

The lights, which hang from long cables from the mall's roof, contribute to visually reducing the height of the main building and giving it a more human scale.

Eurospar
Leibnitz

Architect	**Riegler Riewe Architekten**
Location	**Leibnitz, Austria**
Photograph	**© Paul Ott, Graz**

The Eurospar in Leibnitz, as envisioned by Riegler Riewe, was designed to be the epicenter of an extensive region that would quickly reap the benefits of the commercial momentum the supermarket encouraged once it was up and running. The aim was to build the best supermarket possible using Eurospar's corporate identity, the color red and a translucent, highly efficient exterior structure.

The supermarket welcomes its customers with a spectacular glass wall that spans the entire length of the building's front facade. Inside, the logical arrangement of the different display stands and the shelving allows for a clearer distribution of the products, which is simpler and comfortable for the customers. The width of the aisles and the glass facade allow the visitor to visually "enter" the interior long before actually crossing the threshold.

Part of the parking lot is located underneath the spectacular entryway, an extension of the supermarket's roof, supported by columns. At night, or on especially cloudy days, the light from inside the building makes it visible from hundreds of feet away. The center becomes a luminescent cube, surpassing its purely commercial function and becoming an avant-garde architectural space.

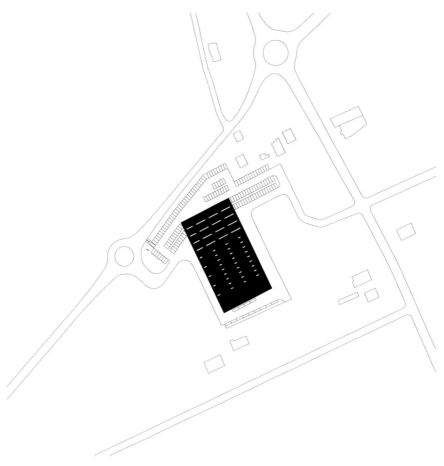

Site plan

In winter, when it is surrounded by snow, the building rises
majestically with an architectural presence that boldly stands out in
its environment but also integrates subtly thanks to its clean lines.

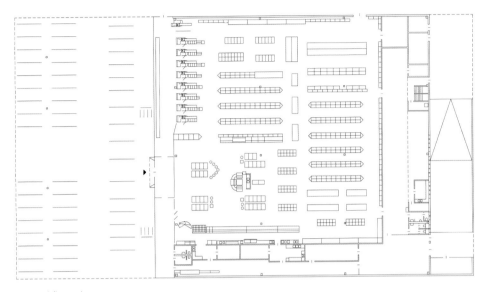

Ground floor plan

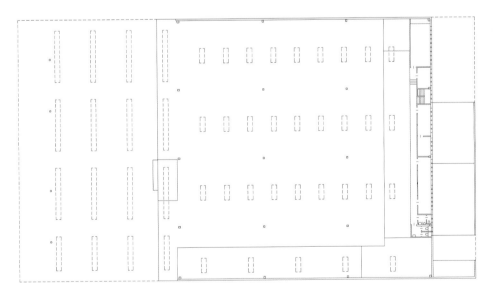

First floor plan

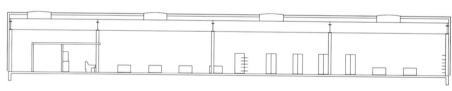

Cross section

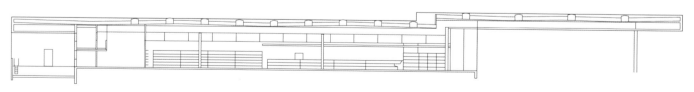

Longitudinal section

The spectacular glass facade welcomes visitors and transforms the
building into a gigantic cube of light.

The building's front canopy has, among others, an eminently practical function: to protect vehicles parked beneath from bad weather.

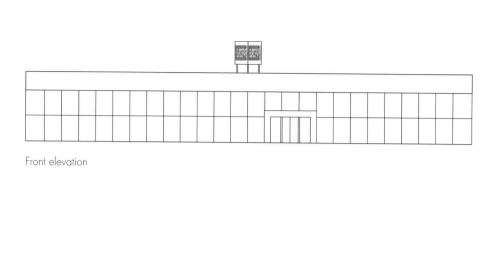

Front elevation

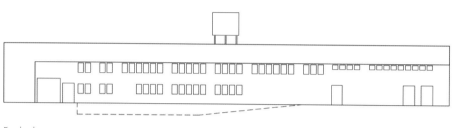

Back elevation

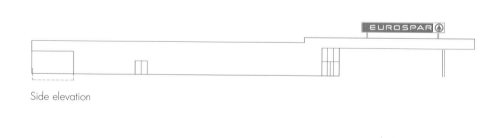

Side elevation

Side elevation

MPreis Zirl

Architect	DPA – Dominique Perrault Architecture
Location	Zirl, Austria
Photograph	© Thomas Jantscher

MPreis is a family-run business with several supermarkets in the Austrian province of Tirol. In the 1970s, in light of the progressive decline and eventual disappearance of small food shops, the company decided to restructure its collection of stores into a chain of supermarkets. Today, MPreis owns several supermarkets in the region, all of which have been designed by prestigious architects, such as Dominique Perrault, among many others.

The MPreis supermarket in Zirl, a small mountain town, integrates perfectly with its surroundings, running parallel to the banks of the Inn River and its adjacent path. This integration is due, in part, to the carefully selected materials used for its construction. The dialogue between the glass and the steel panels on the east facade blurs the distinction between the exterior and the interior of the supermarket. The flow of natural light from outside to inside gives customers inside clear views out, and those outside clear views of the products on display inside. The result is a lightweight building that is not at all visually aggressive and that attains an almost seamless fusion with an environment of incomparable natural beauty. The interplay between inside and out is reinforced by the vegetation on the riverbank, which seems to be trying to enter the supermarket and which acts as camouflage where the building's presence is less subtle.

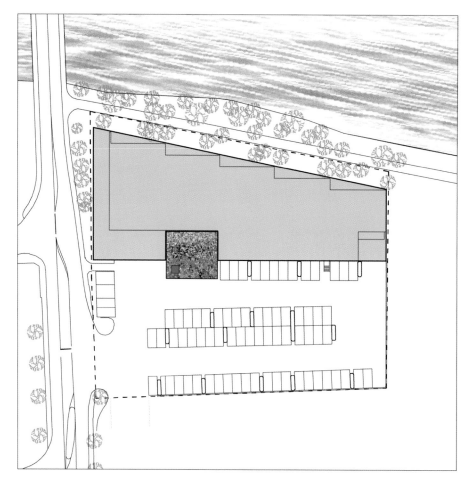

Site plan

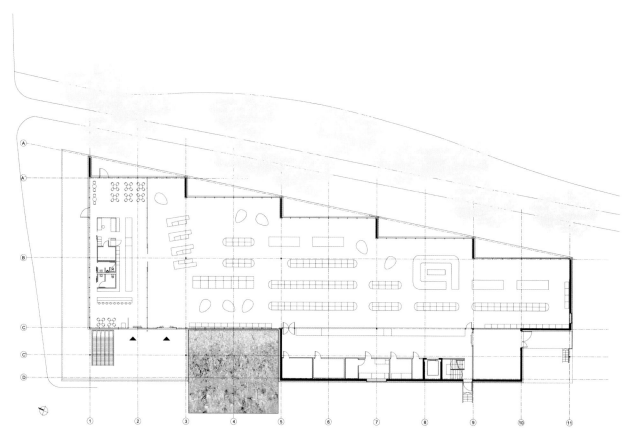

Floor plan

The vegetation that surrounds the building, including the flowerbeds that border the parking lot, plays an important role in the building's aesthetics, softening its presence and integrating it with its surroundings.

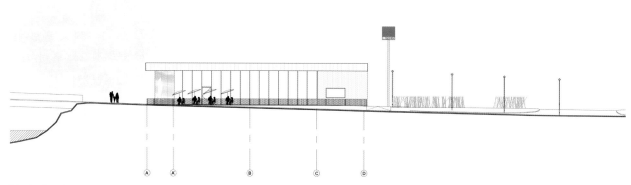

North elevation

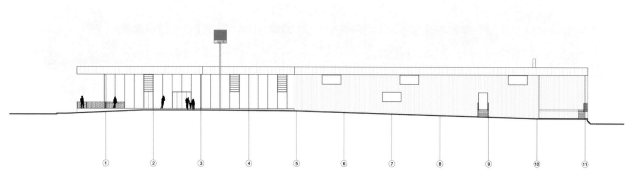

West elevation

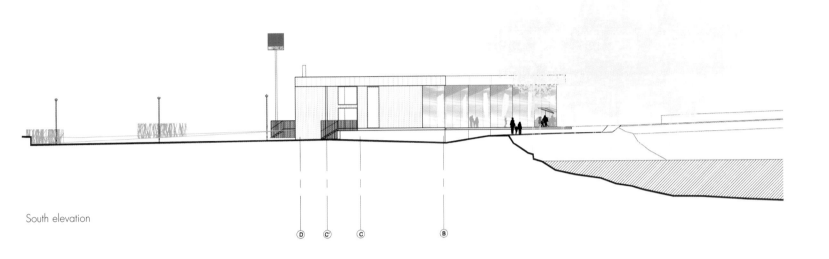

South elevation

Ⓓ Ⓒ Ⓒ   Ⓑ

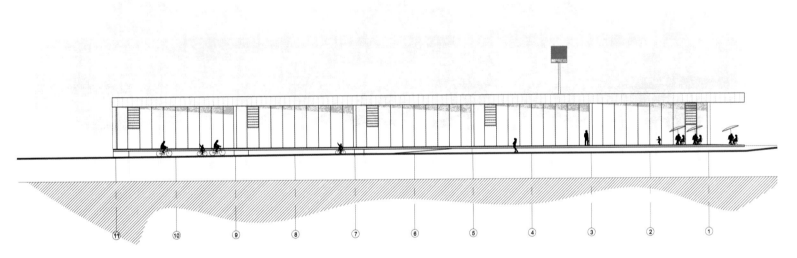

East elevation

⑪   ⑩   ⑨   ⑧   ⑦   ⑥   ⑤   ④   ③   ②   ①

The MPreis supermarket in Zirl runs parallel to the riverbanks, which have dictated its design and given rise to the need to integrate it subtly with the surroundings.

The supermarket's interior has two sources of artificial light: the lights embedded in the ceiling, which provide general illumination, and those hanging from the ceiling, which provide spot-lighting for specific products.

Media Markt

Architect	Studio Fuksas
Location	Eindhoven, The Netherlands
Photograph	© Philippe Ruault

Media Markt is a European supermarket chain that specializes in computer products, household appliances, and audio and video equipment, and has over 24,000 employees and more than 300 stores in 10 European countries: Austria, Belgium, France, Germany, Holland, Hungary, Italy, Poland, Spain, and Switzerland. Its shop in Eindhoven is probably one of the most emblematic and remarkable, from a purely architectural point of view.

The building's main structure consists of a gigantic cube of blue ceramic tiles that connects on one of its sides, via a bridge, with the shopping mall and square, and on another side with one of the city's largest parking lots. From a distance, the three buildings (parking lot, supermarket, and shopping mall) seem to form a single unit, while if you enter Eindhoven from the north, the mall and supermarket seem to form an enormous frame for another of Studio Fuksas's more well-known projects: The Admirant.

The main cube of Media Markt is located above street level, leaving space for the entrance and the windows of the ground-floor shops. Clients who wish to access the shopping mall from the parking lot are obliged to pass through the second floor of the supermarket. This ensures a high number of daily visitors.

The facade's blue tiles have been decorated with a subtle motif that reflects the sunlight in different ways, depending on the angle with which it hits the surface. At night, the sign, which can be seen on the supermarket's north and south facades, lights up. This, together with the nighttime lighting of the shopping mall, creates a genuine light show that gives the square, where the two buildings meet, a strong character.

The building that houses Media Markt is trapezoid-shaped. Its four facades are completely different from one another, giving the building something like a multiple architectural personality.

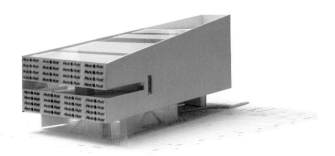

Model of front view

Model of back view

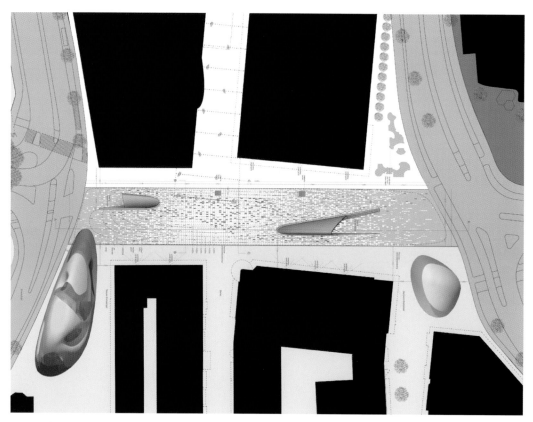

Master plan

The chain's logo is repeated obsessively on one of the building's facades, becoming not just an advertisement for passersby but also another of the decorative elements.

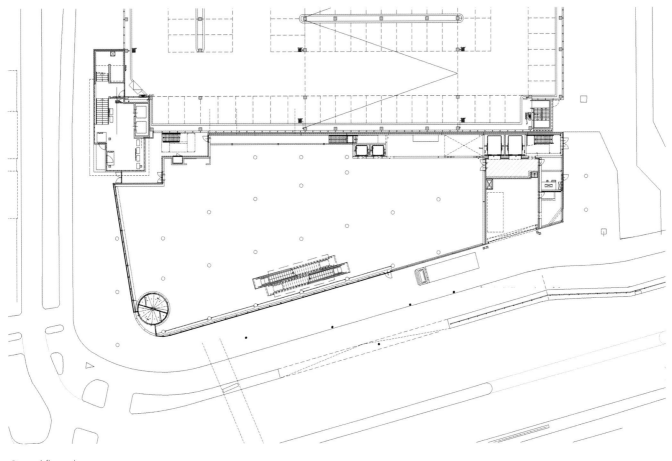

Ground floor plan

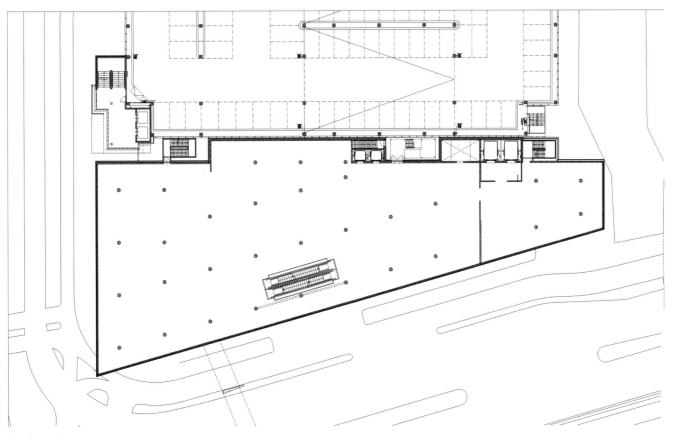

First floor plan

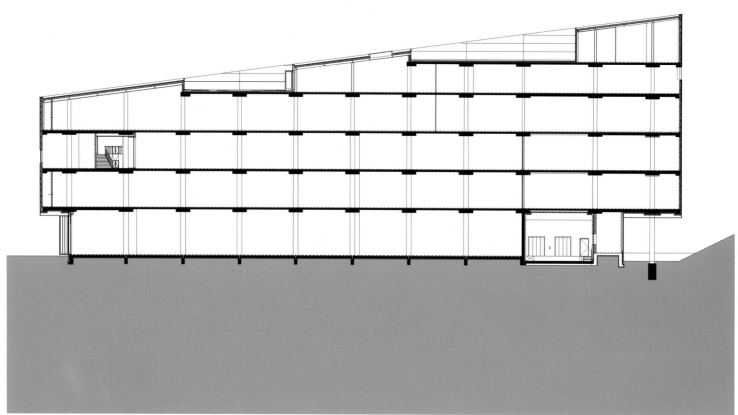

Longitudinal section

MPreis
St. Johann

Architect   **Tatanka Ideenvertriebsgesellschaft**
Location   **St. Johann, Austria**
Photograph   **© Paul Ott, Graz**

The MPreis supermarket in St. Johann, a small mountain village with a population of no more than 8,000 (and hotel room for 5,000 more during the ski season), was planned and designed with the goal of its being converted into the central building of a large commercial area.

The parking lot, built on the first level, below grade, has a roof of prestressed concrete, as does the level above, which is occupied by the supermarket. The roof has been built from beams of wood laminates, with an added covering of XPS insulating panels. The energy needed to power the ventilation and heating systems is extracted from water in the subsoil of the supermarket.

A ramp several feet long connects the ground level to the upper level and allows customers to enter the supermarket without using the stairs. The laminated element that surrounds three of the four facades provides fluidity, thanks to its curved shape, and softens the building's impact on its surroundings.

In the supermarket's interior, the wide aisles and high ceiling suggest comfort and relaxation. The potential for the cold ambience that large spaces such as these have, is avoided here thanks to the large windows, which allow natural light to flood the space, and to the laminated panel, which filters and softens the sunlight, lending warmth to the store's interior design.

Park deck plan

The pillar crowned by a red cube bearing the MPreis supermarkets'
logo allows the building to be located easily from a distance.

The gaps in the front laminated panel allow natural light to flood the interior spaces of the supermarket. The light is filtered, creating a soft effect similar to that of the general artificial lighting.

From the building's interior and from the supermarket's access ramps
there is a stunning panoramic view of the mountains that surround
the town.

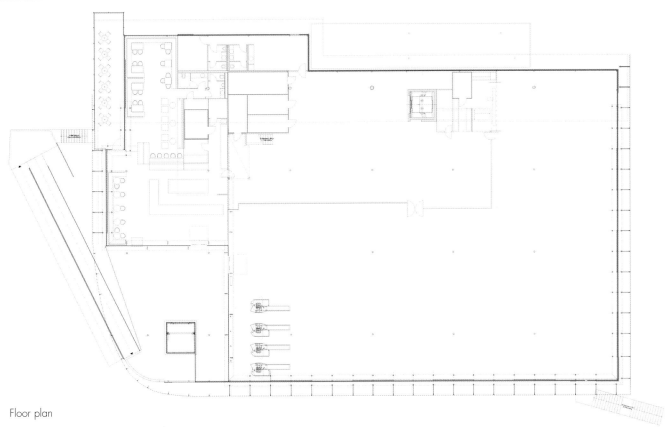

Floor plan

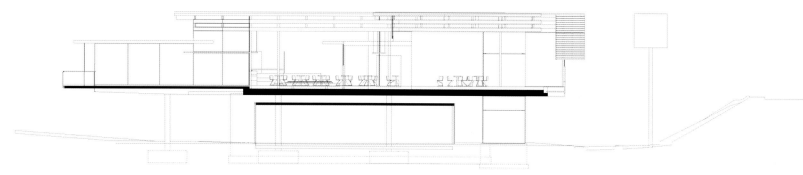

Section

Lidl Mannheim

Architect   **AJR Jörg Rügemer**
Location   **Mannheim, Germany**
Photograph   **© Jörg Hempel Photodesign**

According to Jörg Rügemer himself, "Architects are not obliged to obey their clients unquestioningly; they do have their own point of view." A bold statement indeed, that is not so easy to put into practice when one is commissioned to design a new supermarket for a well-known chain with a strong brand identity, as was the case with Lidl. In this case, the chain asked Jörg Rügemer to create a modern shopping center with a contemporary appearance, which, while eschewing the stereotypical architectural features of Lidl's supermarkets, would clearly respect its identity. One condition, however, stipulated that the supermarket's interior follow the standard layout of the chain.

The final result reduces the use of elements from the company's corporate identity to a minimum. The pitched roof has disappeared to make way for a more ecological structure that reflects its surroundings. The building's design adapts to, and harmonizes with, its context without compromising its purely commercial purpose.

But perhaps the supermarket's most remarkable feature is the exterior facade, comprised of baskets of thick steel filled with limestone and black basalt. The baskets hang from structural elements on the wall and also act as the perfect frame for the wild climbing plants that will cover the building's facade in years to come. The ecological roof, the climbing plants, and the limestone rocks in the baskets contribute substantially to improving the supermarket's environmental efficiency.

The design of the roof's wooden structure is based on an abstraction
of the branches of the trees that surround the building. It is composed
of 51 wooden frames interlinked with steel plates.

The building's canopy seems to rest on the glass cube that welcomes the customer and juts out past the building's structure, marking the entryway.

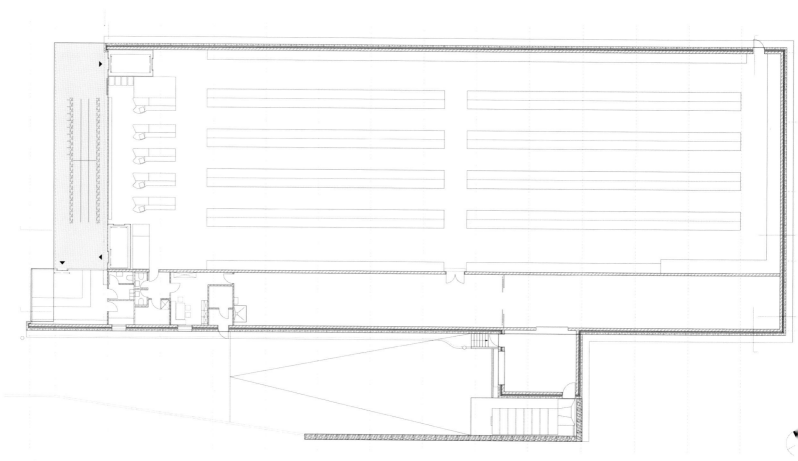

Floor plan

At night, the natural materials that have been used in the construction put the spotlight on the supermarket's interior, which shines brightly and attracts the attention of passersby.

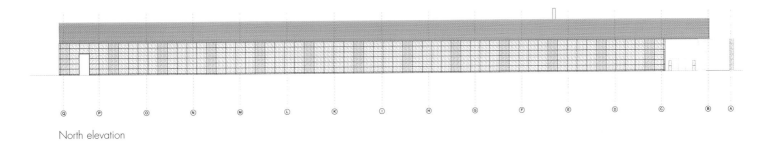

North elevation

South elevation

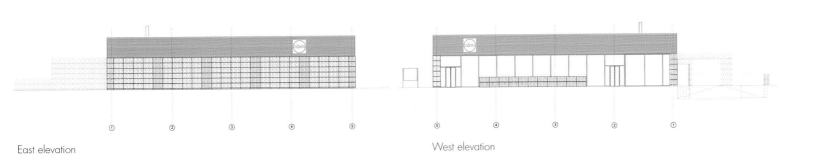

East elevation

West elevation

On the building's perimeter are flowerbeds planted with ivy that will slowly grow and intertwine with the metal grills and stones. In a few years, the supermarket's external appearance will change completely.

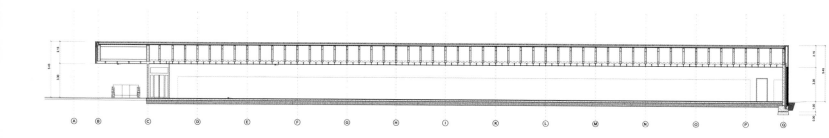

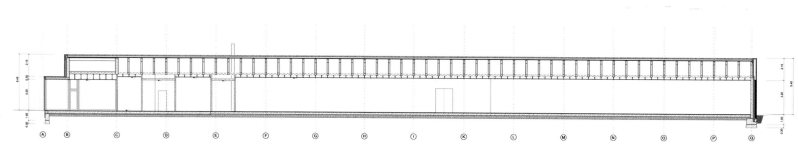

Longitudinal sections

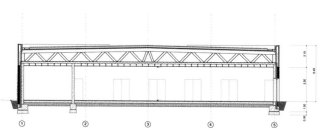

Cross section

In the supermarket's interior, the corporate aesthetics of the Lidl brand
dominate: wide aisles, uniform lighting, and few graphic elements
other than a few posters announcing special offers
and promotions.

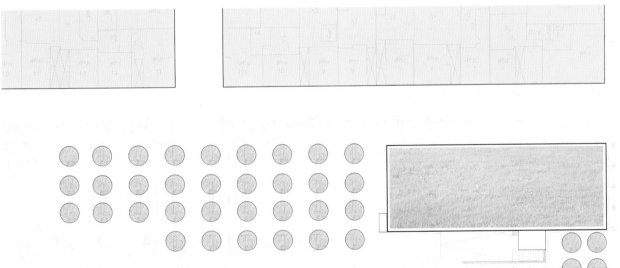

Site plan

Interspar
Schwaz

Architect	ATP — Achammer-Tritthart & Partner
Location	Schwaz, Austria
Photograph	© Günter R. Wett

Described as "a shining silver coat for the city of silver," the Interspar in Schwaz is based on the so-called Corporate Design for Interspar developed by ATP in cooperation with this famous chain of supermarkets. The most striking feature is, without doubt, the shiny silver coat that covers the entire building and that is free of any industrial equipment. The silver roof is, in fact, the supermarket's reccurring motif, and references to it are found in the form of silver thread that runs through the circulation areas, reminding the customer of the city's origins as a silver-mining town. The roof, in fact, has been designed as the building's fifth facade and can be seen from hundreds of feet away. The most spectacular views, however, are those from one of the nearby mountains, where you can appreciate the roof in all its splendor. On especially sunny days, the roof shines brightly, and it is impossible not to notice the building.

The building rises 36 feet high and is divided into different areas: the supermarket itself, where there are hardly any columns in order to maximize the space's flexibility; a raised restaurant, which offers views of both the supermarket's interior and its exterior; the mountainous landscape that surrounds the building; and the Inn River to the north.

Of the four facades, the most important is the one that faces north. Facing the main road that leads to the shopping mall, the north facade shows the spectacular roof "descending" to touch the ground. The south facade faces the central Alps, and offers magnificent views from the raised restaurant terrace inside the supermarket. This terrace is accessed via an outdoor staircase. Finally, the east and west facades have purely functional purposes: The west facade is by the parking lot, and has clearly been designed to offer protection from the sunlight and as a place to display signs. The east facade has the same structure and purpose as that of the west.

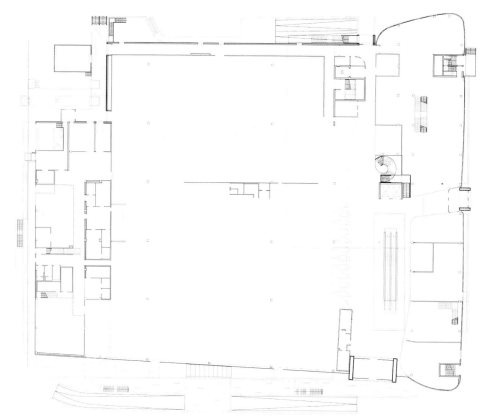

Ground floor plan

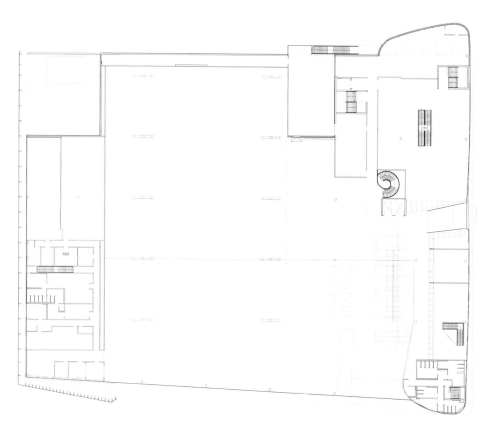

First floor plan

The building has been conceived as an apparently organic space.
The roof unifies the different areas, providing cohesion and a clear
architectural thread that runs throughout.

A large market hall below a sweeping timber roof that rises to a height of 36 feet, almost devoid of columns. This offers great flexibility in the Interspar area.

The chain's logo has been etched onto the building's facade, transforming it into a central decorative element.

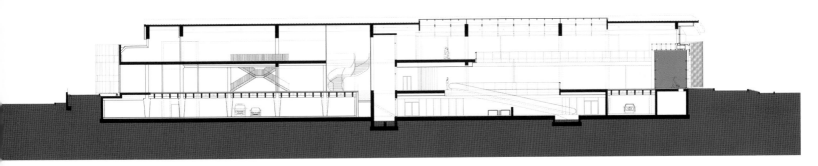

Cross section

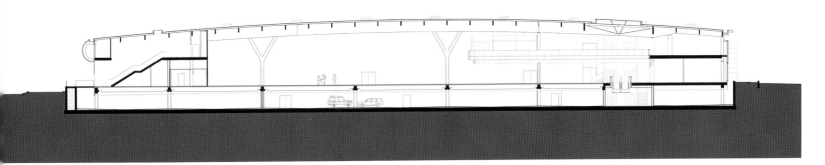

Longitudinal section

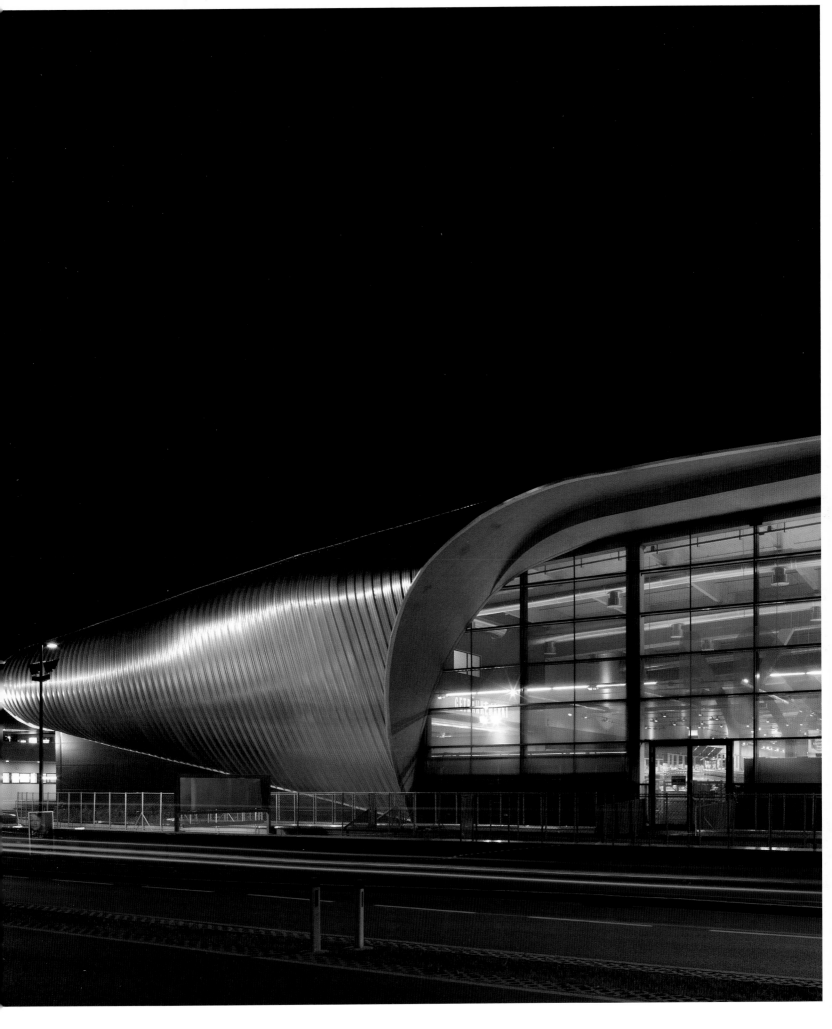

Somerfield
Market Fresh

Architect	**JHP Design**
Location	**Wanstead, UK**
Photograph	**© Adrian Wilson**

Somerfield, Britain's fifth-largest food retailer, has in recent years focused on the convenience market. JHP was the architectural firm chosen to prepare strategic design proposals for three distinct formats. One of them included the creation of a "deli on your doorstep," a high-quality convenience-driven food hall on the natural consumer path of the discerning "food educated" customer.

Their research led to the conclusion that consumers preferred the sub-brand "Market Fresh," that was used on the fascia and the in-store flyer. The aim of this was to capture the interest of the modern-day, cosmopolitan consumer, interested in good quality and fresh food.

The shop revolves around three specialist spaces: Fresh Food, the Deli, and the Wine & Spirits Area. Each of these spaces has a series of distinctive features. Unobstructed windows enhance the colors and the appearance of the fresh produce. Fixtures are kept low to encourage a relaxed market atmosphere of specialist "food" treats. The delicatessen area offers variety, quality, and an exotic flavor. Customers are offered the chance to grind their own coffee or to press their own olive oil. Finally, the wine and spirits area conveys the idea of "authority." Obscure products are demystified.

The supermarket's layout has been executedwith the aim of encouraging customers to wander around the different aisles, creating mini-destinations around the promotional areas. JHP Design also collaborated with Phillips to create a light space that enhances the colors of each and every one of the products on display.

Market Fresh exudes a dramatic and inviting feeling that attracts new customers, who perceive the supermarket as "modern, welcoming, and with a great ambience".

Ground floor plan

Market Fresh exudes a dramatic and inviting feel that attracts new customers, who perceive the supermarket as being modern, welcoming and as having a great ambience.

The wooden panels at the end of a row of shelves mark where
customers can find products on offer and special promotions.

The varying heights of the supermarket's ceiling, which in places
leave the roof framework in view, visually delineate the different
areas of the store.

Special lighting and use of color in the fresh food area brings out
the products' natural colorings—a far cry from the harsh white
lighting found in most grocery stores.

A white frame signals the presence of the supermarket and highlights
it against the red brick facade of the building that houses it.

Photographs of some of the products decorate the store window
opposite the shopping carts. These photographs also offer
the customer an idea of the wide range of products that can
be found inside.